Scuttled

Scuttled

The Sinking of the Palmer Cay

Ron Collins

The author has tried to recreate events, locations, and conversations from his/her memories of them. In some instances, in order to maintain their anonymity, the author has changed the names of individuals and places. He/she may also have changed some identifying characteristics and details such as physical attributes, occupations, and places of residence.

ISBN: 978-0-9988975-0-9

Library of Congress Control Number: 2017901707

10 9 8 7 6 5 4 3 2   0 5 1 1 1 7

Printed in the United States of America

♾This paper meets the requirements of ANSI/NISO Z39.48-1992 (Permanence of Paper)

This book is dedicated to all the former associates of Palmer & Cay that still mourn the loss of "The Ship."

I did not know there was any other way to run a business but to make people accountable, make timely decisions, and service the client.

—Alan C. Greenberg

Contents

Author's Note   xi
Acknowledgments   xiii
Introduction   xv

PART I: The First Year (January–December 2003)
Chapter 1: The Big Leak   3
Chapter 2: New Board Members   15
Chapter 3: The Storyteller   23
Chapter 4: The Ship   29
Chapter 5: The New Skipper   37
Chapter 6: Waves of Announcements   41
Chapter 7: So, What Is an Insurance-Brokerage Firm?   47
Chapter 8: Signs of Change   49
Chapter 9: The Joint Venture   55
Chapter 10: Scoring the PGA Tour   59
Chapter 11: The Benefits Division   63
Chapter 12: The Atlanta Office   69
Chapter 13: New Associates   71
Chapter 14: New Executive Syndrome   79
Chapter 15: The Partnership   87
Chapter 16: Shortcuts to Success   91
Chapter 17: The Big Walkout   95
Chapter 18: Results, or Lack of Results   101
Chapter 19: Bonus Double Cross   105
Chapter 20: You Can't Make More Than Me   109
Chapter 21: A Ghost from the Past   113
Chapter 22: End of First Year   115

PART II: The Second Year (January–December 2004)

Chapter 23: Hiring Mel   121
Chapter 24: Vice President of Everything   125
Chapter 25: Matrix Management   127
Chapter 26: The Disincentive Plan   131
Chapter 27: Tocqueville Society   135
Chapter 28: Failure to Capitalize   137
Chapter 29: The Partnership Meeting   139
Chapter 30: New Atlanta Manager   145
Chapter 31: The Second Vegetable Truck   149
Chapter 32: RIMS   151
Chapter 33: Blowup with the President   153
Chapter 34: Executive Coaching   157
Chapter 35: Strange Happenings   161
Chapter 36: The Wedding   169
Chapter 37: More Jumping Ship   171

PART III: The Third Year (January–May 2005)

Chapter 38: Company Spiraling out of Control   177
Chapter 39: Changes in Attitude   183
Chapter 40: The Godfather Call   189
Chapter 41: My Problems Continue   191
Chapter 42: Palmer & Cay for Sale   195
Chapter 43: A White Knight   199
Chapter 44: Taking on Water   203
Chapter 45: Going Under   207
Chapter 46: The Aftermath   213
Chapter 47: Goodbye, Palmer & Cay   219

Epilogue   223
Cast of Characters   231
Appendix   235

Author's Note

Almost all of the stories in this book are based on my first-hand observations, usually witnessed by others. For any of the stories where my memory may have been in doubt, I went directly to the individuals involved for confirmation. In general, this book represents a chronological sequence of events. Because there were many things going on at the same time and background was needed to provide context, some of the stories may be slightly out of order. Every effort has been made to provide an accurate account of the events that unfolded during this history of Palmer & Cay.

Acknowledgments

For my first book, I turned to a number of people for help and support, all of whom were generous and free with their time and efforts. I would like to start by thanking two special people in my life and the life of this book.

Matt McGuire has been my good friend from the time we met in Washington, DC, many years ago. He became involved with this project when I had only written thirty pages. It was his early encouragement that kept me going. Matt has read more versions of this book than anyone should have to bear.

Donna Burchfield, a longtime friend going way back to our college days at Auburn University, has been invaluable with her support, editing, contacts, and guidance. It is especially helpful to have someone so committed to the project in your corner to keep you going on the right track. Additionally, Donna's husband, Penn

Nicholson, contributed a detailed edit to help me clean up the grammar, punctuation, and spelling.

Along the way there were many people that I imposed on to read the manuscript and voice their opinions. My wife, Jeannie, read and commented on several versions. Betty Barnett was the first person to take a pencil to the manuscript, providing valuable comments and direction. Bill Danish, a former associate, helped me keep the story real. My good friend Hal Rosson in Nashville was an early reader and contributor. My workout partner Tommy Bond was also one of the first to read the book, and his surprise positive reaction was very encouraging. Carol Bowman helped me keep track of and preserve the different editions during the writing phase. My good friend Tom Miller in Texas spent part of his summer going over a draft. Steve Brett was the first person to read the manuscript who had no prior knowledge of the story, which gave him a unique perspective.

Jan Schroder was brought in to provide an outsider's point of view before turning the manuscript over to the publisher. Her fresh eyes greatly helped the readability of this book.

I would like to thank the lawyers of L. Lin Wood, PC, for their guidance, particularly Lin Wood and the very thorough Johnathan Grunberg.

Introduction

Stories that *need* to be told are often born out of tragedy because of the drama the stories present. That's why television news shows start with what went wrong that day rather than with what is uplifting. The story of Palmer & Cay definitely qualifies as drama. This is a cautionary tale with many lessons in the story for future business executives. It's the story of how a 135-year-old, highly successful company could be mismanaged out of business in less than two and a half years, all without a change in technology, new legislation, nor a shift in the marketplace to push it along. It is the story from the inside about the careers, personal lives, and families affected by this almost-unprecedented fall from success.

Palmer & Cay was a commercial insurance–brokerage firm representing corporate clients in their purchase of insurance. Founded in the port city of Savannah with a marine-insurance background and nautical motif for corporate identity, those who loved the company referred to it as "The Ship." In some respects, Palmer & Cay was too good to be true—a great place to work with snowballing success. Good leadership, talented personnel, personal freedom, and generous compensation contributed to the overall success of The Ship. This is a story not of evil wrongdoing, but of runaway egos, greed, and the lack of entrepreneurial skill or knowledge to lead the company forward. Those egos were willing to bet everything on an unproven scheme and ride The Ship to the bottom, if allowed.

So much happened in such a short time that these next forty-seven chapters barely tell the whole story. There were many emotions in the bowels of The Ship during those years, even humor, though it was mostly dark. This is not a big Enron-type story, but one very real and significant to those who lived through the storm. There are a number of business lessons to take away from this tragedy, most of which are of the how-not-to variety. Organizational structure, hiring, compensation, and business ethics are among the lessons. Many may recognize part of their own story in these pages, because no one has total ownership of the mistakes that sank the Palmer Cay.

Scuttle

1. *Nautical*

      a.) To cut or open a hole or holes in (a ship's hull).

      b.) To sink (a ship) by this means.

Part I

The First Year
(January–December 2003)

Chapter 1

The Big Leak

"There will be an important announcement." The first sign of the drama to come arrived on the coldest day of the year, while I was sitting in an old, drafty, Victorian-style club in downtown Richmond, Virginia. Even though I had anticipated the weather by wearing a sweater under my wool sports jacket, the room was so cold I kept pumping my legs up and down under the table in a useless effort to generate heat. I was so distracted by my discomfort that I almost missed the most important revelation of the last two days. I'm not sure what we were discussing when Ray mentioned there would be an important announcement next week in Atlanta, and then, looking directly at me, he added, "In fact, you will really like it."

Flippantly, I asked, "Why, Ray, are we selling the company?"

Before he could respond, his partner, Dave, shut down the conversation and Karen, our chief financial officer (CFO), chimed in that he had already said more than he should. Wow—from their response and the look on Dave's and Karen's faces, I could tell this was big, whatever it was. The conversation then drifted to other topics, as if I was the only person in the room who had heard what Ray had said. None of the other half dozen attendees seemed to notice or care what Ray was talking about. From that moment on, I no longer thought about frostbite or heard the floors in the old mansion creaking as the servers went about their business.

Reflecting on the loose lips during cocktails and dinner, it occurred to me that if Ray just let that slip, I could have gotten the entire news out of him over a couple of whiskeys. Ray liked to talk and be the source of company gossip, an authority on all subjects. Yet there was no way now I would get him alone, and after this session we all would be flying back to our home cities. The fact that Ray directed his remark toward me was especially intriguing, because he and I had never been on the same page since Palmer & Cay bought Ray's company, Slabaugh, Morgan, and White, a few years back.

There had always been an awkwardness below the surface between us. It was a matter of style. Ray Slabaugh was almost ten years older than me but several generations apart, an old-school executive whose management approach was stuck in the 1960s when form was favored over substance. Everything was "feel good" then, even if it meant misleading employees. Ray had not adjusted to the evolving changes in the relationship between management and the workforce. Back in the '50s and '60s, man-agement held up carrots to the employees in the form of promises of pay and promotions while at the same time being much more invasive into the personal lives of the employees. Everything was subject to discussion, from facial hair to marital status. People were expected to go along with whatever management decided was best for them. They were expected to work many hours beyond the normal work week to include early mornings, evenings, and weekends. If the company said transfer, your response was to be "What city?"

Ray was also the stereotypical micromanager who conducted interminable meetings to go over and over the same topics. Did he suspect from our strained relationship that I secretly was ready to see us sell the company? Since he was on the board, he must've known how much my stock would be worth at current multiples.

No, I thought, *that can't be it.* I had never given anyone any indication I wanted out. Plus, Ray was a master of gathering all the data and coming to the wrong conclusions, including about my personal career goals. Contrary to his open pronouncements, I did not want and was not competing for his job. I planned to retire in five or six years in my current position. Then again, if the sale price were large enough, I thought selling could be an attractive option before my retirement.

The rest of our quarterly meeting droned on without my participation. Something big was up, and I had no interest in the mundane issues that would still be on the table when we had our next meeting in three months. Afterward, waiting for a cab outside in the sun was actually warmer than the meeting room in which we had just spent two chilly days. My clenched muscles finally started to relax as my body warmed. At that point I was barely communicating with the other managers sharing the cab to the Richmond airport. I couldn't help but wonder, What possibly could be going on in the company that, as a senior officer, I was totally unaware of? After all, I spent time with the chairman and primary owner, John Cay, almost every week. Atlanta had become the flagship office of the company and John worked closely with all the senior managers and producers in developing new business. John was always our best new-business developer. We all knew if he made an introduction to a new prospect there would be a good chance of getting that business. John was always forthcoming about news within the company. In fact, he would answer any question you asked. His answer a number of years back about selling the company was "Fortunately, we can do this work for a long time." He meant that we were not limited by age. John was two years older than me and really enjoyed building the company—so much so that I was afraid he would never sell the company and retire. The company was 135 years old with twenty-one offices and close to one thousand employees. I had no reason to think that John was in any hurry to see it end. Plus, insurance brokerage will probably be around as long as there is a need for commercial insurance. After all, someone needs to keep the insurance companies straight.

On the flight, I decided a couple of drinks between Richmond and Atlanta would help me sort things out. Perhaps because I *did* want to cash out, or maybe because I could not think of any other news pertaining to the company that would make me any happier, I started thinking that the company was really being sold. What else could it be? Like a person buying a lottery ticket, I started thinking about what I was going to do with the money. It would not be enough to qualify as "go to hell" money, but life sure would be more comfortable for my wife, Jeannie, and me. We could pay off the mortgages in Atlanta and at our house on Lake Burton. How much should we put away for the kids' education? We should give something back in the form of charity. What about upgrading cars? As a former Porsche owner, the Cayenne had my interest. Jeannie's SUV was getting worn, and we both had improvements in mind for the lake house. I hoped that it was my time to score a big hit like I'd seen happen with so many friends and others who had struck it rich when their businesses sold.

By the time the plane hit ground in Atlanta, I had convinced myself that selling the company was the only thing next week's announcement could be about. Over dinner that night I shared my thoughts with Jeannie, who would also be happy with the sale of

Palmer & Cay. She knew how I felt about my current situation at the company, working with "Command and Control" Ray, who really did not represent the collaborative culture encouraged by Chairman John Cay and President Mike Crowley. Things had reached the point that earlier in January while John was out of the country, I mentioned to our president, Mike Crowley, that when John returned I wanted to discuss getting out of management and returning to full-time sales. At the time, only 14 percent of my compensation was for management duties, while most of my time was devoted to running the department. When I tried to pass off some of my business to my account manager, whom I was grooming for sales, John indicated that he did not want to pay both her and me for business I produced. Mike's reaction to my comments seemed strange at the time, since he asked no questions about my thinking. Instead, with a knowing look, he simply said, "Don't do anything right now." In hindsight, he obviously knew something was about to change. Over the weekend my thoughts never strayed very far from what was about to happen.

Monday morning was a long time coming. Even though I had been awake for hours, I arrived at my office at the usual time. As was my normal routine, I made the rounds on the twelfth floor to visit with my staff. Monday was my favorite day because many of the conversations were more social than business at the beginning of the week. Everyone would talk about their weekend and their families. Tuesdays through Fridays were mostly about business. This habit of visiting with everyone stemmed from a management concept I picked up back in the nineties called "Management by Walking Around" (MBWA). This style created a strong bond with my people and kept my finger on the pulse of the department. These informal get-togethers allowed people to bring me up to date on what they were working on, ask for my help, or get things off their chests.

Then it was upstairs to check in with the rest of the Atlanta office. The space upstairs was configured like many white-collar businesses; windowed offices on the perimeter with workstations in the center forming a circular pattern on the floor. I usually started in the executive area and worked my way around counterclockwise. The goal of this round was to find out what others in the company were working on and to see if there were any opportunities for my people to get involved in new business. The first office was John Cay's. On this particular day, he was not in, which was not out of the ordinary; his main office was in our headquarters in Savannah. Most weeks he would show up at least once. John was always in and out thanks to the small jet that we kept in the air so much we had had to replace the engines.

Continuing my tour of the office I stopped and visited with, or at least said hi to, everyone who was there. Since most of the people in offices were in sales it was not unusual for many to be out or late making an appearance. I had my usual stops: Doug Hutcherson, Phillip Holly, Chuck Gehrke, Tom Bennett, Fran Millar, Phil Maddox, and the last stop before the reception area, Tom Coker.

Tom was the VP in charge of the general administration of the office. He managed the administrative staff, receptionist, mailroom, and other noninsurance personnel. Tom also managed the budget, approved expense accounts, and performed annual reviews on about half of the staff. Obviously, he was in a position to know what was going on. I settled myself into one of the chairs in front of his desk and we exchanged the happenings of the weekend. Eventually the conversation came around to the goings-on within the company. Neither of us had much to report, so I asked him if he had heard anything about a corporate announcement. "Nope," he replied.

"Has anyone reserved the main conference room for a meeting this week?"

"No, why do you ask?"

"Slabaugh let it out in the meeting in Richmond last week that there would be an important announcement coming. And the response from Dave Morgan and Karen Lehman was like 'Oh shit!'"

Tom's face lit up. "Maybe John is selling the company."

Tom had made a big hit once before at a previous company and, since he rolled much of his money into company stock, was looking to have an even bigger score when Palmer & Cay sold. Palmer & Cay stock was privately held, with a new valuation conducted by an outside firm each year. In recent years, the stock valuation had increased in giant leaps of 25 to 50 percent per year. John Cay and his family owned a little over 50 percent of the company, the rest owned by current and past employees. The stock was not publicly traded. Professional-level employees could buy in (no free stock or options), and we all stood to do well at retirement—or when the company was sold.

I headed back downstairs to my office with no work on my mind. Little did I know this was only the beginning of the "no work" days, of which there would be many in the months ahead. "No work" days were days lost due to emotional stress fueled by events or conversations with fellow employees. The loss of production caused by the changes in the company would be immeasurable.

In between phone calls and discussions with various members of my department, I tried to figure out what was going on. Just before lunch, I decided to make a few calls to see what turned up. First, I went right to the top and called John Cay's office in Savannah, feigning I had something to discuss. As expected, he was not there. His secretary told me he was traveling and would be back at the end of the week. I then asked her to transfer me to Karen Lehman. She was traveling to Atlanta. Next, I called Richmond and asked for Ray or Dave, the coleaders of my division, and lo and behold, they both were in Atlanta. It seemed like everyone important in the company was coming to Atlanta—perhaps for an offsite executive committee meeting.

Nothing happened the rest of the day. That night I went home still not knowing what in the hell was going on.

* * *

Tuesday was pretty much a repeat of Monday: everything quiet in the office with everyone going about their business. Everyone, that is, except for me. Coker and I talked, neither one of us having any news.

Then, on Wednesday morning, Katie Tidwell, one of our account managers, casually walked into my office. "What do you think of the new president?"

By the look on my face, she knew she had me. I had no idea what she was talking about. It could not be Palmer & Cay! We had a president—Mike Crowley, longtime insurance executive who was liked by everyone in the company!

"Katie, new president of what?"

"Yeah, Palmer & Cay. The guy from Marsh."

I immediately knew something was wrong. Marsh was the biggest insurance broker in the world, and I was certain John Cay would never sell to them or bring in someone from Marsh to take over his company. I was so confused that it never occurred to me that maybe we had been bought by a private-equity firm and it had planted one of their own to take over. That scenario would not have been a bad outcome if the sales price were high enough to make us all happy. As I would soon find out, that wasn't the case either.

"Where did you hear this?"

"Gary heard it from one of the insurance reps who calls on Marsh."

I quickly headed down the hall to find Gary Edwards, the producer that Katie assisted. "What is Katie talking about?"

"That is what I heard! We have a new president, a guy from Marsh."

"What's his name? What about Crowley?"

"Didn't recognize the name. He's not from Atlanta, that is all I know. You need to ask your friend John Cay." Gary laughed at his little remark, knowing fully that with how much time I spent with John, I was one of his go-to guys. We both understood this change in management was serious.

When I got off the elevator on the fourteenth floor, the news was already making the rounds. The buzz had started, but no one knew any details. As you would expect, people were gathering in small groups to tell each other what they didn't know. No real news other than "We have a new president who worked for our major competitor" circulated. This was not what I thought was going to happen, and to say I was worried would be an understatement. My first instinct was to wonder if our 135-year-old insurance firm really needed a new president. We were very successful with our current management. Why hire a new coach in the middle of a winning season?

Everything for the next two days was a blur of conversations, mostly unsubstantiated rumors. Many people were not happy. We liked the company the way it was, and we were all loyal to Mike Crowley. Tom Bennett, always a relatively fast-talking person, was speaking at a new land-speed record. He was *really* unhappy. In typical Bennett fashion, he had already performed some research and was ahead of the rest of us.

"Don't know about you, but I don't need a big-company guy trying to make us into a Marsh. Besides, I don't like the way Mike is being treated. There is nothing wrong with the company the way we are!" he said. "By the way, did you know this guy Jim Meathe was fired by Marsh? Go on the Internet and check him out. The Marsh people have nothing good to say about him."

Coker was bewildered; the rest were in shock. Most of us had come from big national firms before joining Palmer & Cay. We all felt the same about the joyless bureaucratic companies managed out of New York or Chicago—companies where salesmen were just street soldiers. Now we would have one of their castoffs as our boss.

And what about our current president, Mike Crowley? Being that the primary owner, John Cay, was still very active in the business, Mike had been the perfect fit for our closely held company. In those circumstances, it takes a certain temperament to be successful. Mike was a true Southern gentleman from Richmond, Virginia. Actually, he had the temperament of a good golfer, which he was, having played on the golf team in college. In those days, Mike had played alongside future professional golfer Lanny Watkins, which made for a good background to be an insurance executive. He was kind and fair with everyone and could be counted on when help was needed. Having previously worked for a national insurance broker, Mike shared our management philosophy of touting small-company values and personal freedom. Once, in a pre-budget-planning meeting, some of the younger managers tried to show their management acumen by coming up with new reporting for expense accounts. Mike stood up (just as I was coming out of my chair) to end the discussion. He said we didn't need more procedures or forms; we were at Palmer & Cay to get away from big-company ways. Mike was good for the company, and we did not need anyone else. I really liked working for him, as did most of the other senior managers.

Thus, my initial reaction to this unsettling news of the new president left me feeling a little guilty. On one hand, I was as disturbed as everyone else about what I was hearing; however, at my age, if ramping up our congenial little firm with a more aggressive posture would lead to greater personal wealth, I could be interested. The company was doing so well financially . . . was I being selfish for wanting to get more out of it for my eventual retirement? I knew I could not share my deeper thoughts with anyone in the company, and for that I was uncomfortable. Looking back later, I realized that what I was thinking was probably the same thoughts that drove John Cay. The difference was that John could and did act on his feelings.

What was really perplexing was that this move was so out of character for John Cay. An abrupt management change without forewarning was not his custom. He was always open and direct about his plans, which was one of the reasons, as my wife pointed out, we trusted him. Trust was an important issue because Jeannie and I, along with many other families, were investing heavily in company stock that was not liquid on the open market. Our confidence in John and the company was so strong that one year I borrowed several hundred thousand dollars from The Savannah Bank to buy stock. Fortunately, we were growing at such a pace that I made that money back in just two years. Up until now, there had not been a surprise agenda.

Another reason we were all confused was that John's hands-on management style would not allow for a new executive to come in and make wholesale changes. So, what would be the purpose of bringing in a new president? When Mike Crowley was first brought into the company, he was not allowed to buy pencils without John's permission. What about this new president would be different? To those of us fully engaged with Palmer & Cay, none of these changes made sense.

From time to time the company would bring in management-consulting companies to provide guidance to our management group. Usually the consultants would show up with a two- or three-day program featuring their proprietary approach to their area of expertise. They would have their charts and outlines with exercises for the group to complete, each consultant thinking they had solved some big management dilemma. John would go along with the program for about a day and a half before totally losing interest. He would then abruptly end the training, which caused great consternation on the part of the outside advisors. They would object and try to continue, causing things to get testy. In one situation, John announced that he had things to go over with the management team and made the consultants leave the room. In that case, we passed on the final day of training. Knowing John's history when involving people from the outside, it was hard to imagine an outside, new president having any say in the operation of the company.

Chapter 2

New Board Members

Conversations moved so quickly over the next few days that I am not sure where I heard the official company line. Basically, John brought in two outside board members and reshuffled the management team. Up until that point, the board had consisted of John Cay, the chairman, Mike Crowley, the president, two of John's old friends who were outside members from the business world, one salesperson, and the rest were senior Palmer & Cay executives. In the new formation, the board was reduced in size and most of the company-employed board members were dropped from the group. The two outside businessmen, both close friends of John's, would remain. Mike Crowley was promoted—or demoted, depending on your point of view—to vice chairman.

The two old friends of John's were Joe Rogers and Don Chapman, both prominent in the Atlanta business community. Joe was the chairman, president, and primary owner of Waffle House, a well-known Southern institution that, in most states, can be found every twenty miles along the interstate. Don, a huge Georgia Tech supporter, had owned Tug Manufacturing (the vehicles that tow airplanes to and from the gates) and a large optical retail chain. Don became very wealthy over the years when he sold the companies. I had met both men and always felt good about their influence over the company. They were both hard-nosed businessmen who created cultures in their own companies that would have been too restrictive for my liking. However, I felt certain they would help John keep us out of trouble. John's ambition often led him to consider business deals that concerned the rest of us on the executive level. Once when we were still a small company, John wanted to buy a London insurance broker. Another time he had me fly with him on the company plane between Charleston and Atlanta in order to have an uninterrupted conversation about taking on a third-party administrator (TPA) that some business group was trying to unload. They were willing to give it to us at no charge. Obviously, this administrator was not making it in the boondocks of Central Georgia. I said, "John, no one gives away an ongoing business of any value. They probably have liabilities they could not walk away from." Fortunately, John heeded my advice and we passed on this situation.

Joe Rogers's father and a partner founded Waffle House back in the fifties. Selling basic breakfast food is a very low-margin business that must be strictly managed. Joe grew up in the business, literally working every job. To this day, even top executives are required to work holidays to keep their hands in the business and to give employees time off. On Christmas and New Year's Day I have found Joe Rogers, the chairman, working behind the counter in various stores in the Atlanta area. Although Waffle House corporate works hard to stay out of the press, there are a number of stories from past executives and employees that have made the rounds over the years. One rumor that is particularly telling about the culture is that Joe once wanted to fire a secretary for throwing away an envelope. Supposedly, the CFO at the time stepped in to protect her. From my own experience, I knew that Joe blocked the purchase of disability insurance for the executives for a long time because he thought they may malinger if out of work for health reasons. Also indicative of Joe's hands-on management style was that he insisted on personal site visits for every new restaurant location before giving the approval for construction.

Don Chapman did not appear to be as extreme as Joe Rogers, just a tough, practical businessman. I did not have much exposure to Don or his companies, but there was one instance that gave me more than a clue to his management style. John, Joe, and Don all belonged to an organization called Young Presidents' Organization (YPO). Some people referred to YPO as "Your papa owned it." Anyway, to be a member you must be a president of a company at a young age. John asked me early in my Palmer & Cay career to make a presentation to his YPO group about the future of employee benefits, especially group health insurance. When I got around to the projected cost of health-care plans, Don Chapman leaned back in his chair with his hands behind his head and declared, "Hell, I just want to hire employees, not adopt them!"

With these two men on the board, I felt fairly secure about the future of the company. However, there was one safeguard missing. For years, Lew Oden had been the executive vice president of the company and John's right-hand man, inherited from his father's time. Lew had retired in the last few years and was totally disengaged by now. John may have been the visionary, but Lew was the control. It was Lew who evaluated everything that was put forth to John, and there was plenty to look at. Palmer & Cay was the target for everyone trying to sell their company or looking for a good place to land. Our reputation was the best. We had grown during my time from around $12 million in annual income to approximately $140 million. That was in just fourteen years. Our employees at all levels were happy, all the insurance companies were competing for our attention to choose their products, our clients respected us, and all the big insurance-brokerage firms wanted to buy us. We were the second-largest privately owned commercial-insurance broker in the whole country and proud of it. John Cay's personal wealth was growing at over $1 million a month. What could go wrong?

In the past, time after time, I watched Lew put on the brakes when John wanted to go forward. There were all kinds of crazy schemes or people looking for inflated compensation. Lew had the ability to sort out the pretenders. He would also renegotiate deals that people thought they had made with John. That was always fun to watch. For example, closing the acquisition of Slabaugh, Morgan, and White (SMW) took many months because Lew and our CFO, Karen Lehman, would not sign off on the deal without thorough due diligence. SMW was a group made up of recently acquired small insurance agencies in Southern states. Or, as my good friend Tom Bennett would say, the company was "a bucket full of minnows." Most of the offices were either not profitable or underwater. Had there been a real due diligence earlier, they would have known that the manager of one office spent his days taking music lessons. In another office, the manager lost his major client and basically was through. Payroll as a percentage of income was high (a bad sign), and most of the employees—including former owners—did not know the company was being sold. What a mess! Even after closing the deal, we never totally merged the books in order to keep an eye on what was going on in the new offices.

People were always approaching John about joining the company with unreal expectations of income. In one situation, I watched Lew negotiate a salary down from $20,000 per month to something under $10,000. That individual made the mistake of thinking that when John did not object to his salary request, his actions amounted to consent. Wrong!

At the time, no one appreciated the critical fact the Lew was not there to shepherd the deal that John had struck with the new board members. While I believed in their business acumen, Joe

Rogers and Don Chapman had no experience running a financial-services company like Palmer & Cay. In business enterprises such as financial services, accounting, law, insurance, stock brokerage, etc., the accepted logic is that the inventory goes down the elevator and leaves the building every night. In other words, the people selling knowledge, advice, and services are the business, as there are no tangible products or hard goods being sold. The culture in our offices was totally different than managing a restaurant or welding metal or selling eyeglasses. We would soon find out how different.

So, who were these two new board members? John Gussenhoven and Joe Platt were both former partners of another insurance broker known as Johnson & Higgins (J&H). John Cay had known John Gussenhoven from his school days at the University of North Carolina (UNC). Gussenhoven was a nice-looking guy, dressed well, and flew his own jet. He had recently contacted John Cay about a business venture he was promoting, and that initial conversation led to discussions about the future of Palmer & Cay. Per John Cay's own words to me, Gussenhoven and his close friend Joe Platt would affect changes in Palmer & Cay that would result in a two-phase growth spurt. First, we would go from $135 million of revenue to $300 million in two years, and then to $500 million by the end of five years. That would be phenomenal growth, unheard of in our industry without acquisitions. In return, each of these men would receive a small ownership position in Palmer & Cay.

I got the feeling that Gussenhoven may have been in a circle of people during college that John Cay either looked up to or wished to join. Back in the sixties, UNC was where many well-heeled Southern families sent their offspring for education. It has always been interesting to me how many business and civic leaders of my age in Atlanta are graduates of UNC. I am sure with so many high-profile, high-achieving students, the social pressure of peer groups may have been more pronounced at Chapel Hill than what would normally be found at other institutions. Of course, social pressures can be found anywhere. Was John Cay's connection with Gussenhoven a holdover from school days when Gussenhoven may have held sway over John Cay? Was John Cay still viewing Gussenhoven through the same lens as when they were young men? I don't know the answer to these questions. All I know is that in fourteen years, I had never seen John defer to anyone else when it came to running the company.

Joe Platt, on the other hand, was physically thick with a square, meaty face. He looked more like he could have been an enforcer in a big city up north. On the surface, bringing in these two guys made no sense to me. Not only were they coming from a culture totally alien from the entrepreneurial organization that always had been Palmer & Cay, but their previous company, Johnson & Higgins, was reportedly not in a good financial situation when it was sold. Right after J&H sold to Marsh, I had the opportunity to talk with a former employer of mine who was president of a national firm that had bid on buying J&H. To my surprise, he said that because their numbers were so bad, the partners of J&H did not have much choice about selling the company.

To get an idea of how different J&H was from Palmer & Cay, you need to know some background. J&H was a unique form of partnership that was grandfathered under the law. At one time, they were considered by most people as one of the best companies in insurance brokerage and consulting. The company was owned by a group of partners, usually around twenty-five to thirty-five in number. Becoming a partner in J&H made a person very wealthy. People would describe their partnership meetings this way: "They cover the floor of the board room with one-hundred-dollar bills, then the partners enter wearing golf shoes and get to keep the money that sticks to their spikes." What was not an exaggeration was the disparity between the partners' compensation and that of the troops. Management was able to use the company's reputation in the marketplace to hold down salaries. At one time, everyone wanted to work for J&H, and many were willing to sacrifice financially for the experience. Obviously, somewhere along the line things went bad either from greed, mismanagement, complacency, or some of all of the above.

Palmer & Cay, on the other hand, had been owned by the Cay family and allowed the professional-level employees to buy shares to the point where almost half of the company was employee-owned. The only outside shareholder was a former employee, Jack Kingston, the well-known congressman from Savannah. For the most part, Palmer & Cay was a sales organization with formula-based compensation. Typically, the formula included a percentage applied to your block of existing and continuing business, and another percentage applied to new business. There was no limit; you ate what you killed! At any time, I could figure out my compensation with a pencil and one piece of paper—two minutes max. You always knew where you stood. It was a transparent culture. That was the beauty of Palmer & Cay.

Then suddenly, we had two new board members from a troubled, bureaucratic, national firm guiding us. These new board members, more than anything else, would set into motion the fatal leaks in The Ship. To make matters worse, we would later find out that these two each had a $5-million, no-cut contract. That's right, six zeros even if the company failed! Lew Oden would never have allowed that to happen. What they offered in return was to take Palmer & Cay from $135 million of revenue to $500 million in five years. The bottom line for John Cay seemed to be money. Growing his wealth at $1 million a month was not enough. Phil Maddox, one of our producers, claimed that John wanted to join the billionaire club and upgrade our little executive mailing tube to a full-size Gulfstream jet.

Chapter 3

The Storyteller

Before going any further, you probably should know who is telling this story. I am the former Senior Vice President and Managing Partner of the employee-benefits division of Palmer & Cay's Atlanta office. I was born in New York at the beginning of the baby boom right after World War II. My grandparents on my father's side were Irish immigrants who settled in New York City. My father worked his way through New York University before joining the army during World War II. My mother's family in Italy were from the public-service class of teachers, lawyers, and government workers. My father became a career army officer, reenlisting after the war. My mother was born and raised in Italy, meeting my father when she was a typist for the US Army.

While my dad was on active duty, we moved around the world every three years. His final assignment was in Huntsville, Alabama, while I was finishing up high school. Due to proximity and at the urging of a newly met school friend, I chose a Southern university for my college education. Upon graduating from Auburn University, one of my roommates asked me to be in his wedding in Atlanta. Atlanta, being the closest major city to Alabama, was very enticing. After a brief brush with graduate school at the University of Alabama (I really had an undergraduate attitude), I headed straight for Atlanta to find work.

My first job was with an insurance company as a trainee in the group-insurance field office. After almost a year of training, I was sent on the road to Alabama and Tennessee, calling on insurance agents and brokers to sell them on the idea of using our products for their corporate clients. I finished my first full year in the top ten countrywide for group disability-insurance sales. My reward for good performance was a transfer to Boston, where I moved in during a snowstorm and suffered through a fairly bad winter. That was not where I wanted to be, and things were not working out professionally for anyone in our office, so I resigned with a break from work and California on my mind.

On the way out west, I visited friends in Atlanta. While there, I was contacted by one of the national insurance-brokerage houses and talked into a job, with only two weeks off for my California visit. The next three years were a good lesson in hard work that set the foundation for my career. Wanting to get into a management position, I took a job with a small life-insurance company in Washington, DC, affiliated with a large automobile insurer. At the ripe old age of twenty-eight, I was the director of group insurance. The title was more impressive than the actual responsibilities; however, it was a real management position. Two and a half years of home-office experience was enough for me, as the environment was very different than working in the field selling group-insurance programs. Even though as an executive I had unlimited personal leave, I found reporting to the same place every morning boring. When the opportunity presented itself, I returned to Atlanta with another national insurance-brokerage firm.

It was the experiences of the next eleven years that grew my appreciation for working with corporate clients at the highest level. In employee-benefits brokering and consulting, the client contacts are usually the people in the C suite, typically the CFO, CEO, CHRO, or even the president. Representing clients in the insurance marketplace was challenging, stimulating, and rewarding work. I loved my job, and after three years was promoted to manager when my predecessor transferred to another office. Hiring, training, and growing the staff was also satisfying. Over the next seven years, we grew the group department from four people to seventeen and achieved the Large Group Office Award and National Office of the Year. In typical large-company fashion, there was no celebration in Atlanta for our accomplishments, and the bonuses that year for my staff were smaller than the bonuses when we didn't win any awards. On top of that, the senior management group in Atlanta felt shortchanged by a new bonus program created during tough economic times. Finally, the atmosphere in the Atlanta office was more than many of us could take. Even though I really liked my work, the situation became unbearable and, like a number of other department heads, I moved on. I became intent on finding a less bureaucratic environment to further my career.

My next move was to a small entrepreneurial firm headquartered in Savannah with a small outpost in Atlanta. I was the twenty-first person hired in the Palmer & Cay Atlanta office. In the beginning there were three of us in the benefits group. When hired, I was told there was around $200,000 of revenue on the books. I figured that the number was probably closer to $120,000. When I got into the books, I discovered that the number was under $100,000, closer to $90,000. Not much to start with, but we had some early successes and were able to double the revenue number in each of the early years. Fifteen years later, we had forty-eight people and close to $10 million of annual revenue. This represented a great deal of hard work by everyone, but never seemed to be drudgery.

Along the way we had a great time, and our benefits group and the Atlanta office as a whole became like family. We were the small boutique company competing with all the major players, creating much success. This feeling of family was pretty much the same throughout the Palmer & Cay offices, which is why this story about The Ship is so dramatic.

Why did I choose to spend my professional life in the crowded, competitive field of insurance brokerage, where the barrier to entry was only to pass a state insurance exam? Selling for insurance companies, which is how I started, is a very task-oriented business where you prepare proposals, negotiate terms, close a deal, and then move on to the next opportunity. In that role, you are essentially a wholesaler calling on agents and brokers to use your products for their clients. Each year you start with a big "zero" by your name and begin again only with a much larger goal. Eventually management gives you a nut too big to crack, which is one way they control your compensation expense. Sooner or later, the law of geometric progression sets in and you can no longer reach the targets for the incentive compensation.

By contrast, as an insurance broker/consultant, you are on the retail side of the business. You are an outside advisor to corporate management, an extension of their business. It is not a one-and-done situation; you develop an ongoing relationship with your clients. In that role, I always felt I was really part of the business community. The people I met and worked with were often leaders in the community. The competition may have been fierce, but not everyone was capable of the sophistication required to work at the highest levels. For the larger clients, group insurance is a complicated financial transaction, usually the second- or third-largest expense for the company behind salaries and raw materials. Clients often treat insurance-company representatives as outsiders that can be plugged in or replaced at will. As a broker or consultant, you sit with the clients in making those decisions as part of their family. This is a much closer personal relationship more to my liking.

On the personal side, I married later than most (age forty-seven) to a beautiful, younger woman from Stone Mountain, Georgia. Jeannie worked for an insurance company when we met, and we were together for four years when we tied the knot. That was 1994, my fourth year with Palmer & Cay. Thirteen months later we welcomed our daughter into the world, and then eighteen months after our daughter, our son arrived. My father had passed away earlier that year after a tough fight with cancer, so we named my son after him. As soon as the kids were out of diapers, we added one more member to the family: a yellow Labrador retriever named Sophie. Sophie quickly became a beloved member of the family.

While Jeannie was pregnant with our son, we moved from a small 1960s-ish brick ranch house to a much larger house of the same era two miles from Peachtree Street. We made the move in 1996, the year of the Atlanta Olympics, thinking that with a larger house we could accommodate any relatives from Italy that might want to visit during the games. That was a great plan, but unfortunately, it was not to be. We nonetheless enjoyed our new, rambling home, which, like the old one, was only several miles from my office. Being close to the office made for an easy commute, but the downside was that it also made it far too easy to stop by the office on the way home from the airport after a business trip. Also, it was tempting to go in for a few hours on the weekends, which was a habit I was trying to wean off of after starting a family.

Living in Atlanta for most of my adult life offered a great deal of stability that I did not experience growing up in a military family. Early Friday evenings were usually spent at a watering hole with the same friends that I would jog with on Saturday mornings. Jeannie and I always had one evening each week designated for Mexican food at a favorite restaurant. After the children were born, we still tried to have one night out for ourselves. Jeannie's parents, sister, and extended family were close by, and my parents lived in Huntsville, Alabama, a three-and-a-half-hour drive from Atlanta. Many of my friends from college lived in Atlanta or Southern cities, and many of them traveled through Atlanta fairly frequently. For vacations, Jeannie and I both enjoyed the different beach communities around the Southeast. Although we lived in a big city, we felt a real sense of community in Atlanta. In my mind, life was pretty comfortable in the Palmer & Cay days.

Chapter 4

The Ship

So what about Palmer & Cay? Actually, at the time I joined it was known as Palmer & Cay/Carswell, a result of buying out the largest competitor in Savannah. When purchased, the John D. Carswell Company was larger than Palmer & Cay. The patriarch, John Carswell, was getting up in age with no family members interested in taking over his company. Both Palmer & Cay and The Carswell Company were longtime mainstays in the Savannah business and social communities. Savannah, like Charleston, its sister city up the road, was very provincial at the time, before retirees started to move into the area. The joke was that just being born there did not necessarily make you a native. In order to be considered with due respect, you needed to have a traceable bloodline back to colonial times, preferably back to England.

The chairman and CEO was John Cay III, a direct heir of the founders of the firm. John's great-grandfather had been a baseball player at Georgia Tech in Atlanta who passed up professional baseball (financially an easy decision, since back then the pay was not so great) to join his father-in-law's insurance agency in Savannah. The firm was passed down through family members, and one day John's father announced that he wanted to retire. Either John could take over the firm, or Dad would put it on the market. John eagerly took over the reins with ambitions way beyond Savannah.

Although I never met John's father, Jack, my understanding is that he was the typical Southern patriarch, almost a caricature. He was a man's man, a hunter, someone who enjoyed a drink of brown whiskey and a ribald story with the guys. The father was a bigger-than-life guy, liked by most. Although John did all the right activities—hunting, golf, and tennis—he was only a very casual drinker, had no interest in fine dining, and never, ever used profane language. He was always in control and totally driven in business. It was reported by those who knew the old man that he would make fun of young John's speech, which probably was affected when he attended the University of North Carolina. Jack would say, "I paid money to send my son to college to learn to say 'outstanding' instead of 'no shit!'"

The single-office insurance agency in Savannah would never be enough for John, even if it was highly profitable. I was first exposed to John's ambition early on when the two of us traveled to Nashville to meet with several prospects. One of the companies we called on was the stock-brokerage firm J. C. Bradford & Co. After our appointment with the risk manager, John asked to see Mr. Bradford, the head of the firm. When we were ushered into his office, we found a distinguished-looking Southern gentleman sitting behind a classic wooden desk in a conservative but well-appointed office. I could tell by John's reverence in speaking with this man that John was talking to his role model. J. C. Bradford had offices all over the Southeast, and John let Mr. Bradford know that while we only had a half-dozen offices at the time, we intended to keep growing.

An interesting aside to my first trip with John Cay happened in flight that early morning. John called the flight attendant over and ordered two whiskeys. My first reaction was, Are we going to drink with breakfast? When the attendant returned, John threw the two miniatures into his briefcase. He repeated the same routine that evening on the way home. I would come to learn that John was not a drinker, but frugal. He flew so much that he was always in first class and might as well receive the accompanied benefits. This supported my feelings about his conservative leadership, which I appreciated. A number of years later on a visit to our headquarters in Savannah, John and I were to meet some people at the Savannah Yacht Club for dinner. John wanted to stop by his house to change and offered me a drink while I waited. He opened the closet in his den, where there were hundreds of airline miniatures.

By contrast, in the firm I was with before Palmer & Cay we had an account executive submit a budget for travel and entertainment (T&E) of $55,000. That was more than the head of the office spent, and this young guy had no out-of-state clients. He and his few clients were living off the expense account. I was glad to get away from that culture. At Palmer & Cay, you were expected to use good judgment when spending company money.

John was the classic case of someone who was more interested in making money and growing the business than spending money or living lavishly. No mistake about it, he was extremely driven. Some people put forth the idea that John was trying to prove himself to his father to earn his respect. I didn't buy that and wrote it off to pop psychology. Ambition is in people's DNA, and John had more than most. When we would reach a stated goal such as a revenue level, John would quietly change the goal and move on without comment. When I first arrived at Palmer & Cay, the goal was $25 million by '95. When we reached that goal faster than anticipated, suddenly the target became $50 million. I remember thinking I was the only one who noticed the change. This increase in company ambition would repeat often over the years.

John saw himself as a mover and shaker in the business world and tirelessly devoted himself to that image. John actually lived the life of an over-the-top, hardworking, busy executive to which Jim Meathe pretended. A typical day for John might've been an early-morning flight on the company jet from Savannah to Columbus, Georgia, where we had a very successful office with major accounts. After breakfast with clients or prospects, John would fly to Atlanta to make calls, which might or might not include lunch. Late in the day, a quick flight to Charlotte, North Carolina, or Richmond, Virginia, would not be unusual. On some days, he might end up back in Savannah for a civic or society event that evening. When working with John, managing his schedule was always a challenge. He would overbook himself, not allowing enough travel time. Often you would find yourself running after him from the parking lot to catch up in the lobby of some building at the elevator bank. With him, there was always a yellow legal pad with a "to do" list covering the entire page. I had never met anyone so disciplined in his use of time. That discipline extended to his approach of problem solving. He resolved any problem that might otherwise slow down his efforts as efficiently as possible in order to focus back on the journey to success. Sometimes that might mean spending more money than called for just to get an issue or person to go away without a long, drawn-out conflict. This was an essential component in Palmer & Cay's success: we could make decisions quickly and efficiently.

Above all, one characteristic was key to John's success: he had no call reluctance whatsoever. He was not afraid to get in front of complete strangers and ask for their business. Many people avoid asking friends or acquaintances for their business, but John had no problem with that either, pulling it off with grace and Southern charm. One morning John strolled into my office and wanted to know what I was doing for the next few hours. When I replied that I planned on catching up on paperwork, he responded, "Get your coat on. We're going to call on Coca-Cola." He was not talking about some local bottler out in a rural area, and in a few minutes I found myself downtown, sitting in the lobby of the Coca-Cola world-headquarters tower across the street from the Georgia Tech campus. The night before, John had apparently been seated at dinner next to the president of Coke. There is no doubt in my mind that during the course of the evening he asked the man for the "opportunity to earn" the insurance business at Coke. John was fond of saying, "Give us your toughest problem to prove ourselves." The response given to John was that Coke was looking for minority firms to do business with, probably as a result of recent adverse publicity. Of course, like all the other firms in Atlanta, we had several minority-partner relationships carefully built just for this kind of situation.

In addition to his compulsive work style, John, like many of the people in the communities of Savannah and Charleston, was a total anglophile. His work dress would have fit in on the streets of London, and he drove the British Range Rover in Savannah. At work, he often wore bow ties with striped suits and on the tennis court, long, white pants. You get the idea. In my mind, he resembled a skinnier version of Prince Charles, thinning bald spot and all. Once, he left the US to spend a year in London under the guise of establishing better relationships with the Lloyd's of London brokers. It was on Good Friday that John went to work out at his London club. Since it was Easter weekend, many people had left London, leaving only a few people at the club. While John was by himself, the doors opened up and Lady Di and her bodyguards walked in to use the facility. Taking a break at the water cooler, John introduced himself to the princess. Her reply after inquiring where he was from was "Oh, Savannah, that's where they make the G5." At least she knew her luxury jets. The next day there was a phone message at home from the club noting that they were aware John had spoken to Lady Di and asking that he refrain from doing so in the future. John's wife, Mimi, was horrified at John's breach of protocol, while John just shrugged it off. He would approach anyone who came within close proximity.

In taking over the firm, John inherited his father's right-hand executive, Lew Oden. This would prove to be an important factor in the firm's success. They formed an effective team: John the visionary and Lew the analytical counterweight. John thought in terms of big ideas and Lew would figure out how to achieve John's goals. It became a close professional relationship that would serve the company well for many years. As luck would have it, their combined efforts did not start off well. The first attempt at expansion was to open an office down the coast in Brunswick, Georgia. It was fortuitous that they started in a smaller community, because it was not a smooth start. Evidently, they brought in the wrong person from the Brunswick community and eventually had to start over. Fortunately, Brunswick was not an expensive mistake, and the shaky start did not derail their plans for expansion.

The company benefited in many ways from being headquartered in Savannah. First, there was an abundant supply of educated people who were willing to work for wages below what the big national firms were paying in New York and Chicago. Second, people from elsewhere whom we wanted to impress (clients, vendors, and possible acquisitions) wanted to travel to such an attractive, entertaining city. Then, in the late nineties the book *Midnight in the Garden of Good and Evil* came out, giving Savannah much publicity. In fact, John Cay and his wife, Mimi, attended the "Married Women's Card Club" described in the book. Palmer & Cay also employed a member of the Sonny Seiler family mentioned in the book. Sonny Seiler was the breeder of Uga, the bulldog mascot of the University of Georgia that can be seen in his custom-made jersey on the sideline of home football games peering out of his air-conditioned doghouse. John and Palmer & Cay were very big fishes in a small pond.

One of the things that came with being an important player in a small community was the contact with celebrities. During the 1996 Summer Olympics, John escorted the famed journalist Walter Cronkite around the sailing venue. In 1999, when John Travolta was in Savannah filming *The General's Daughter*, he rented John's house on the water. John owned a plantation across the river from Savannah, so renting out his primary residence was no problem. Then there was the time that John's secretary answered his phone to hear a man's voice ask, "This is Ben Affleck, is John available?" Her response: "Yeah right, who is this?"

As a result of a series of mergers and acquisitions, the company could trace its roots back to 1868, right after the Civil War. The company brochure produced in the mid-1990s had a picture in the inside cover of Robert E. Lee sitting at a table with former Civil War Confederate General Joseph E. Johnston. Johnston was the officer famous for leading the Confederate retreat from Atlanta during the war. Like athletes of modern times when their careers are over, General Johnston sought a career in business and wound up in insurance. That was the last known picture taken of General Lee. That picture remained in the brochure until we quoted on the insurance for a large, well-known minority contractor in Atlanta.

The company logo was the SS *Savannah*, the first steamship to cross the Atlantic. This nautical theme harkened back to the days when the company, based in a seaport, was mainly focused on marine insurance. People felt the logo was a classic symbol for the company and mostly spoke with reverence of The Ship. The Ship was on everything we touched, from the cover of the brochure to koozies to keep your drinks cold. I especially liked the blue ties with the gold repeat pattern. Very classy!

In the four previous companies of my insurance career, I had never worked for an organization so devoid of politics as Palmer & Cay. People generally got along and worked together for the common good. It was an invigorating, refreshing atmosphere. Company gatherings were something to look forward to, usually including outside activities (golf, fishing, boat rides) capped off with food and drink. A good time had by all. Our own little haven that, like all good things, was not to last.

Chapter 5

The New Skipper

The first step for our new board members was to bring in their man to show us how it's done. That man turned out to be the previously fired Marsh executive, Jim Meathe. Of course, everyone scrambled to see what they could find out. After all, a high-profile person with the world's largest insurance broker should be fairly easy to trace. He was easy enough to find, but what was harder to discover was anyone willing to say nice things about him. The Marsh bulletin board on the Internet was full of negative comments about our new president. Apparently, he made many enemies along the way. The Internet wasn't the only place to check him out. I called my Atlanta counterpart at Marsh to see what he knew.

"Don't know him," he said, "but certainly have heard about him."

"What did you hear?"

"Big ego . . . no one likes him. He will leave a trail of crushed dreams and broken careers."

Great, just what we all feared. Some big-company guy who would bust our chops. And, as we would later learn, he had the same $5-million, no-cut contract as the other two new board members. With this knowledge, it was increasingly harder to keep an open mind about the changes in the company. Lew would have put a stop to this. Now we were obligated for $15 million to three strangers from an alien business culture while the people who built the company were kept in the dark, unrecognized and not consulted.

The meetings started almost immediately, some off site, others in the main conference room. The meetings were on a need-to-know basis, and most of us were excluded. This caused a great deal of speculation, hurt, and an enormous amount of "no work" days for everyone. Finally, after two weeks of this, I caught John Cay alone in his office and told him I wanted to meet the new president.

He looked at me like this was a total surprise. "You haven't met Jim yet?" I wanted to say something sarcastic but bit my tongue. He informed me that Jim would be in town the next day and he would introduce me.

My anxiety level built overnight as I waited to meet this person who would have a dramatic impact on my company and my career. After lunch the next day, I headed upstairs to meet the mystery man. When I got to John's office, the door was shut, and I didn't want to be seen lingering in the hallway. As I started to leave, the door opened and out flowed John and Jim Meathe with his wife and young son. I wasn't expecting a crowd, so I knew immediately any hope for a meaningful conversation was shot. My first impression, I would later learn, was the same as everyone else's: he looked like Rick Moranis, the actor. Short with wavy, dark hair and glasses, in his forties, Jim Meathe was not at all what I expected. I anticipated a tall, balding, lean, hard-as-nails, serious-as-a-heart-attack-looking guy. I was looking for Jack Welch (former head of GE), and instead we got *Honey, I Shrunk the Kids.*

I did not pay much attention to his wife, whom I would later learn was a lawyer. Since I did not have any first-hand knowledge about the man, I just hoped Jim was not about to star in *Honey, I Shrunk the Company*.

What did we find out about why our new president was fired from the world's largest insurance broker? At the time, he was head of the Midwest region, which included large offices like Chicago and Detroit. Marsh, being the largest commercial broker in the country, had accounts like Motorola and at least one (or maybe all) of the big automobile companies, along with many of the best-known American companies headquartered in Ohio, Illinois, Michigan, and surrounding states. He certainly had one of the largest regions of the country, a position that placed him near the top of the company at a young age. Part of his success was tied to a group of people working in his region who latched onto a new approach for corporate-owned life insurance (COLI), which made an enormous profit before the IRS clamped down with regulations. Life was good for Jim, so what happened?

As always is the case with high-profile firings, there was much speculation. Mainly, it sounded like he was an uncontrollable maverick. For example, by his own admission, he once hired former Secretary of State Colin Powell to deliver a speech for a regional meeting to the tune of $100,000. No matter what company you work for, regional VPs don't have the authority to spend that kind of money without corporate knowledge and approval. Evidentially, Jim must not have thought that applied to him. Another example along those lines was the remodeling of the Chicago office. Because of the opulence, it was quickly nicknamed the Taj Mahal. Jim must have liked marble. Much later I learned from a credible witness who was also a senior executive at Marsh the probable reason for his dismissal: he had become so contentious in senior management meetings that he became disruptive to the point that people were incredulous of his behavior. In corporate America, being right or thinking you are right will only go so far if people can't work with you. Jim Meathe was not bigger than Marsh.

Jim's lifestyle should have been a warning of things to come. Right from the start, Jim's big-spending ways were not in sync with the down-home Palmer & Cay culture. He insisted on staying at the Ritz-Carlton down the street from the office instead of the Marriott or DoubleTree next door. In the evening, he would have meetings with fine dining and $100-plus bottles of wine. High-end living was convenient in the part of town that housed our office. Buckhead is the upscale part of town known for shopping, dining, the Governor's Mansion, several country clubs, and the home of Palmer & Cay's Atlanta office.

By comparison, John Cay had no use for fine dining and would look for ways to avoid those meals unless clients were involved. Once when we were hiring three people as a group for my department, Jim insisted on hosting breakfast at the Ritz, where the cost for breakfast was more than evening meals in most places. At that time in Atlanta, power breakfasts were held at the White House Restaurant farther south on Peachtree Street—sausage, eggs, and grits under ten dollars. Everyone at Palmer & Cay watched and waited to see how John would deal with this high roller.

In an attempt to control Jim's expenses during the transition from Chicago, John made Jim start staying at his personal condo south of the office on Peachtree Street. John probably figured that temporarily sharing his private, two-bedroom space was better than having him running up expenses at the Ritz. Yet from all reports, the change in residences did nothing to tamper down the expense-account dining. This became a trend that I would observe of other new members of the management group.

Chapter 6

Waves of Announcements

When the announcements began, it was a torrent:

- *Palmer & Cay announces the appointment of National Property Insurance Leader*
- *Palmer & Cay announces National Sales Leader*
- *Palmer & Cay announces National Aviation Leader*
- *Palmer & Cay announces National Workers' Compensation Leader*
- *Palmer & Cay announces National Surety Leader*
- *Palmer & Cay announces Northeast Regional VP, Midwest Regional VP, etc.*
- *Palmer & Cay announces new offices in Detroit, Columbus, Cincinnati, Chicago, etc., etc., etc.*

There were too many announcements to keep up with. They almost all had two things in common: the people were from outside the company, and they were usually from Marsh. It was as if all the hardworking people that helped grow Palmer & Cay into one of the best insurance-brokerage firms in the country didn't exist. Apparently, these big-city boys from other parts of the country were going to show us Southerners how it was done. Sounds like the beginning of a joke: "A Yankee and a Southerner walk into an insurance agency . . ."

Yet we knew something that the new people didn't, especially those of us who came from national firms. The truth was, clients often chose to go with Marsh because no client executive is ever fired for choosing the world's largest insurance broker. After all, they must be doing things right. Palmer & Cay was tiny by comparison, so we earned every new account by working harder and smarter. We never went into a sales situation with the attitude that it was a given that we would get the account. The new guys were oblivious to what was going to change in their lives. There was a lot of pain ahead.

Before the reorganization, Frank Beard had been in charge of most of the commercial-insurance division. In effect, he was the number-three person in the company. One day, I walked into his office to find Frank visiting with another executive, Ruffin Branham. When I asked how it was going, he faced me with a whimsical look and threw the piece of paper in his hand up in the air (some meaningless form) and said, "I get to do this." We all laughed hard, but the truth was not funny. Senior executives reduced to clerical work. How things had changed.

When I look back on those days, it was as if we were part of a family where the parents divorced and, after our father remarried, we had new siblings whom we did not know. We had strangers living under our roof who received all the attention, while we felt taken for granted. Nothing we could do would restore us to our rightful place, and only by leaving might we get noticed.

One thing about Jim Meathe: at times, he could be so self-absorbed that he would unknowingly telegraph his moves. Most of the time if he was thinking something, it just came out with no filter. Once, early on, in an after-dinner address to around one hundred of our employees, he referred to Palmer & Cay as a "pissy little company." Another time at a small dinner gathering, someone asked his opinion about the business book *Good to Great*. He responded that he liked the book but disagreed about what the author concluded regarding the leader's role in creating success. One can only presume he was not in agreement with the level-five leader described in the book as a humble executive with tremendous work ethic. I am sure he thought his persona, in lieu of grinding hard work, was the most important thing that would lead us to success.

The one announcement that was of particular concern to many of us was about a national sales manager. In the past, that role was left to the president of the company. Now we would have a dedicated person, which conjured up images of some twelve-hour-a-day person hell-bent on riding to success on the backs of the sales force. Everything would be timed, measured, followed up, and analyzed as if we were machines in a production line. This announcement came soon after I interviewed a sharp, young guy who wanted to leave one of the large mutual-fund companies where he was already earning an outsized income. When I asked why he wanted to leave that job to go into the insurance business, his answer was telling. He was burnt out! To begin with, we had a hard time setting the appointment for the interview, which was unusual because salespeople always have the personal freedom to take time out for interviews. Not this young man. At his current job, he was required to have a minimum number of sales appointments per day that, at times, made it logistically difficult to go from one to another. Then, immediately after each appointment, there would be a call from the home office to the prospect confirming that the sales rep had been there. Talk about a Big Brother situation.

My guess is that the new sales manager would be implementing some kind of time-management system that would require each person to account for every hour of the work day in increments of fifteen or thirty minutes. I had worked under one of those systems in a past life, which is where I learned creative writing. I did not want to go there again. By this point, we were all anticipating the worst.

In addition to the apprehensions that most of us had about the new organization, there were several Palmer & Cay people who thought they should be in consideration for the national sales-manager job. One was Doug Hutcherson and another, Fran Millar. Each was very successful in commercial-insurance sales. Doug wanted to come to work at Palmer & Cay so bad that when we wouldn't hire him in Atlanta, he got himself hired in our Charleston office, became successful, and then transferred to Atlanta. He would go on to produce the largest account ever sold in the Atlanta office. And yet, passing over current employees for key positions would become a pattern in which most of the opportunities were handed to the newbie outsiders.

Fran Millar had always wanted to be in management, and when his previous employer had chosen someone else for the sales management job, Fran left the company. When the employer held back compensation, Fran sued them twice for a number of reasons. The suits lasted several years, with Fran settling for an amount in excess of a million dollars. Not a bad outcome.

Needless to say, the announcement of a national sales manager from the outside did not go over very well with many of us, especially with Doug and Fran. Doug said to me on several occasions, "Cay just turned over the keys of the company to these guys." From about that time forward, Fran would not refer to John Cay without the condescending nickname he devised: "JC three sticks" (John Cay III). Things were starting to get ugly.

It would be several weeks before I got a look at the new national sales manager, Bill Lenhart. One day, word was passed on to me that the new guy was upstairs for a meeting. When I exited the elevator on the fourteenth floor, the main conference room adjacent to the reception area was empty, so I turned left down the hall toward the executive offices. There in the waiting area, speaking on the telephone, was a young man who could have been mistaken for a college intern. With his short, brown hair and chubby cheeks, he looked to be in his twenties. I was sure I had clothes older than him. Only the quality of his suit and shoes differentiated him from a student. All I could conclude was that this guy must be something special, a dynamo, like someone you would read about in a Grisham novel, first one in before daybreak and the last to leave after dark. *This,* I thought, *will change our whole environment. Palmer & Cay will no longer be the pleasant place to work.* Everyone I talked with had the same impression: anyone that young who was appointed national sales manager must either be something special or a super workaholic.

For the most part in those early days, my exposure to the new regime was limited, with much of what I learned coming from the rumor mill. That would soon change in a big way. Amazing how perspective changes when you spend time with people. As my father said many times, "Familiarity breeds contempt." Happily, that isn't always true, but this time it was spot on.

One day, while walking through the reception area, I finally had an opportunity to speak with my longtime friend and leader, Mike Crowley. Our former president was sitting in the conference room by himself, and I went in to shake his hand. Mike motioned for me to sit down. I asked how he was doing and he replied, "Fine." I expressed my concern for the company and don't recall his response. The whole conversation was awkward, since we both knew he was ambushed by John's decision to change directions.

After all, a vice chairman is in the same category as regional vice president. Most companies have them, but they are superfluous positions easily eliminated when the going gets tough. I didn't ask Mike for any details regarding his personal situation and worried that he may have interpreted that as a lack of concern or lack of loyalty. The truth is that I was uncomfortable with everything going on and was still trying to comprehend the situation. I could not think of anything appropriate to express my feelings.

Chapter 7

So, What Is an Insurance-Brokerage Firm?

Along with many other endeavors, commercial-insurance brokerage in the United States mostly developed since the end of World War II. All enterprises that involve property or employees are required either by law, creditors, or common sense to have insurance to protect the assets or cover for liabilities that may result from their activities. An insurance "broker" represents the buyer of the insurance in its dealings with the marketplace. They guide the clients in what insurance to buy for the organization, how much to buy, who to buy it from, and how much to pay for it. This is different from an insurance agent, who represents the insurance company selling the insurance. Even though the insurance broker represents the buyer, the compensation to the broker usually is a fully disclosed commission arrangement paid by the insurance company. In some cases, the broker will work on a fee basis paid by the client.

In the last twenty years there has been significant consolidation in the industry, with a handful of national insurance-brokerage firms buying up many of the local firms across the country. However, there are still hundreds of smaller players in the space and a few regional or superregional firms. At the time of the management changes, Palmer & Cay, the second-largest privately held firm, was known as a superregional, while Marsh, as a result of buying out competitors, was the world's largest commercial-insurance brokerage firm. We were the Porsche of the industry in contrast to Marsh, the General Motors.

The structure of these firms remains fairly universal. They are basically sales organizations led by aggressive producers (salespeople) who trade off of connections, unique knowledge, or price advantage to garner business. Each producer is backed up by one or more account-management people performing the everyday tasks to keep the insurance programs running and the client happy. There is, however, a tremendous difference in the role of management in the smaller firms versus that of managers in the national companies. In the smaller, local firms, managers often double as producers, or at least "rainmakers" of some form. In the large, national, more bureaucratic companies, managers are more into measurements and implementing company policies dictated from above, usually from an executive suite in New York or Chicago. As in almost any other industry, the smaller firms tend to have an entrepreneurial bent, while the national firms operate more in a governmental, top-down fashion.

This distinction between the two types of organizations and their vastly different cultures would have an important role in the events that were about to develop at Palmer & Cay.

Chapter 8

Signs of Change

For good reason, rumors were going all around the company. First, Jim Meathe announced that he would live and work out of Atlanta. This, of course, caused concern for all the finance and HR people located in Savannah. Would they have to move to Atlanta, or would they lose their jobs en masse? What about the legal department and all the other administration people? Would we have two corporate offices? And what about all the Savannah vendors that counted on Palmer & Cay's business? Most of the Savannah staff loved living on the Georgia and South Carolina coasts and had no desire to come to the big city.

Another rumor that began to fester concerned the CFO. From the start, Jim talked about needing a Wall Street–savvy chief financial officer to work with the money markets to accomplish his big plans for the company. How would John Cay deal with this issue? Our current CFO, Karen Lehman, was a hardworking, loyal executive who ran a good, tight department. Whether for budgets, revenues, or expenses, you could count on her numbers. Plus, she was very good at acquisition due diligence. It was not clear why a company with only $135 million of annual revenue would need a Wharton grad/Wall Street type as its CFO.

As I made my rounds each day, it became obvious to me that most people were skeptical of what they had heard. There was a balcony just off the main conference room, and it became routine for me to visit with Tom Bennett outside while he smoked cigarettes. Tom repeated more than once, "I told Meathe not to load The Ship up with debt. For every failed company, there are two financial statements, one beforehand without debt and another after they went out of business loaded down with debt." Tom and I had worked on a number of accounts tied to private-equity firms, and we had both seen the disastrous outcome of being overleveraged.

Still another big-time rumor that was causing consternation was what we heard about the salaries for the new hires. Word on the street was that Palmer & Cay was raising the bar for the entire industry. Of course, all the longtime employees believed it was true, and no one was happy. I decided to once again call Savannah to see what I could find out. No better place to start than with John's secretary.

"Monica, what's the word?"

"Nothing good, that's for sure."

"Why, what's up?"

"John's not happy," she said. "All these new people . . . Meathe is hiring like crazy."

"Rumor is that they are being well paid."

"Yes they are, *very* well paid."

"Is John seeing the offers before they go out?"

I resisted asking her for any specific numbers for a couple of reasons. First, it would have been inappropriate for us to have that conversation, and second, I was afraid of what I might learn if she answered.

"At first he was, but now he just signs the letters and looks the other way."

"How is this happening? John has always been tight when hiring."

"Don't know, but it is not good."

This was so out of character for John, as he had always been a hands-on executive. For instance, once when John passed the concierge desk in the lobby of our Atlanta building, he noticed the many deliveries of the *Wall Street Journal* going to our offices. He immediately changed company policy on who would be allowed to have company-paid subscriptions. He clearly did not believe in throwing around company money. Even John's secretary knew that something was not right, and she had never been afraid to speak up. I would not be the only one to get an earful from her.

* * *

On the morning of the interview breakfast for my new hires at the Ritz, Jim diverted the conversation away from business to explain to our guests what he was looking for in a house. His family was still living in Chicago and would be moving to Atlanta after the school year ended. He was very specific in what he was looking for, and therefore it would be easy for me to remember. That evening I happened to be having drinks with several friends, one of whom was a realtor, Margaret Cox. She was preparing her own family home to go on the market in the part of town Jim desired. When I told her that the new Palmer & Cay president was looking for a house in the area, Margaret began reciting all the features of her house. It was like I was hearing an echo from the morning discussion. She volunteered that if Jim was interested in buying her house direct from her, a portion of the realtor fees could be reduced and she would give him a deal. At around $1.7 million, the realtor fees alone would be close to $100,000.

The next morning, I called Margaret first thing and confirmed what she had described the night before. I put everything down on paper, stuck it in an envelope, and headed upstairs to find Jim. Up on the fourteenth floor, instead of my usual counterclockwise route, I went the other way. I would be able to get to Jim's office without passing his secretary and without him hearing or seeing me coming. As I passed by, I glanced in to see him with his feet up on the desk, leaning back, reading the newspaper. I walked over to Sue's desk and told her I wanted to see her boss. Sue called into Jim's office and then advised me I could have a few minutes of his time, but I needed to be quick as he was extremely busy. When I walked into his office, the paper was gone. I told him about the house, explained the circumstances, handed him the envelope, and then left immediately.

There were three lessons to be learned from this interchange, two immediate ones with the third to follow several weeks later. First, Jim Meathe wanted to present the profile of an extremely over-the-top, busy executive, like in the movies or a TV show. Second, Sue, like many I had seen before, was the executive secretary smitten with her charismatic boss. Not in a romantic way, but rather as his right-hand person whom he takes care of in return. It seemed to me that Sue really believed that Jim was having a busy morning. She moved down from Chicago to work with him and was a close friend of his family. I would need to remember this relationship in my future dealings with her.

The third lesson would come in the form of a phone call two weeks later.

"Hello," I answered my phone.

"Hey Ron, it's Jim. Listen, I just want to let you know that I bought your friend's house."

"Oh, really?"

"Yes, but not from your friend," Jim said. "Someone else took me over there before I could follow up on what you gave me."

What a waste of money. He went through a realtor instead of dealing directly with the owner. Unfortunately, this would not be the last time, either personally or professionally, that Jim would squander money. Months later, I found out that Margaret's house was just the second of three houses that Jim owned at one time in Atlanta. Evidently, when Jim's contractor went to the city to file proposed changes to Margaret's house, the plans were turned down, and that convinced him to buy another house. What kind of person moves to a new city and then buys three houses in succession? I would soon come to believe that Jim was incredibly impulsive about most things in his life. In the many conversations I would have with him, I noticed that he had a habit of interrupting people—including himself.

Chapter 9

The Joint Venture

For two years, off and on, I met with a lawyer from an Atlanta silk-stocking law firm to design a joint venture that could be a game changer for my group. The benefits department in the Atlanta office consisted of twenty-four people in Health and Welfare, eight people in Actuarial Services, four people in Human-Resource Consulting, and seven people in Palmer & Cay Investment Services. We were the largest benefits office in Palmer & Cay, both in people and revenue. We represented approximately 40 percent of the Atlanta office revenue, and often over 50 percent of the pretax profit of the office. In addition to being financially successful, we competed favorably with all the major national firms. This joint venture could blow the doors off, making us the major player in Atlanta.

The project, known as HRvest, was the brainchild of a lawyer named Travis DeHaven with the law firm Troutman Sanders. Troutman was one of the largest firms in Atlanta. The firm's name came in part from Carl Sanders, the former governor of Georgia. Their offices, which were what you would expect from one of the best, were in the tallest building in not only Atlanta, but in the Southeast.

The concept for HRvest was ahead of its time. Since its beginning, a number of law firms across the country, including in Atlanta, have been very successful with what we were about to set up. Palmer & Cay would join forces with Troutman Sanders to offer HR consulting services to major commercial clients. These would be large companies with thousands of employees. Both firms already had a large pool of prospects for this venture. My office alone had over a hundred corporate clients, each with a thousand or more employees. Troutman Sanders had a hundred young lawyers they wanted to keep busy, and Palmer & Cay of course wanted the insurance work.

After many organizing meetings, the name HRvest was copyrighted, an advertising firm was hired, and an operating agreement was drawn up. Troutman Sanders enticed a former partner who had headed up their DC office before becoming the president of a national jewelry chain to return to Atlanta from Dallas, Texas, as president of HRvest. The four-color brochures and accompanying marketing pieces were very professional. Everyone, including John Cay, felt good about the direction we were heading. There was even a catered kickoff event thrown at the plush Troutman Sanders offices overlooking the city. A number of clients and senior members of both firms were invited for this preview. We were off and running, or so we thought.

Since all of the work predated Jim Meathe, and he was not yet full time on the scene, I had John Cay sign the HRvest operating agreement. After all, he was the chairman and majority owner of the company. Who would have more authority than him?

Thinking that our new president would be pleased with such a progressive initiative with one of the most prestigious law firms in Atlanta, I was not worried about going forward. In one of his speeches to the troops Jim once spoke about all the different directions he wanted to take the company. Little did I know what would be coming my way once Jim turned his attention to this project.

Chapter 10

Scoring the PGA Tour

One of the most telling signs of things to come involved the PGA Tour, the sponsoring organization of professional golf tournaments in the United States. Thanks to a connection that one of our producers, Doug McRae, had developed, we were given the opportunity to compete for the group-insurance program of the PGA Tour. The PGA Tour is headquartered outside of Jacksonville, Florida, and they had announced they were taking broker bids. Naturally, everyone in the insurance business wanted the account. Doug brought the challenge to me, and together we started formulating our approach. When our Jacksonville office heard we were involved, they called to tell us not to waste our time. The PGA Tour was a Marsh account, and we did not have enough influence to take it away. Besides, if the PGA Tour did change brokers, the business would stay in Florida, not come to Atlanta. Knowing that the "world's largest broker" would be complacent on such a well-known account (seeing as it was their divine right), Doug and I asked for and received permission to speak directly to the current underwriter at the CIGNA insurance company, which provided the group insurance for the PGA Tour, working through Marsh as the broker. The fact that the underwriter's last name was Marsh (no relation to the brokerage firm of the same name) did not deter us. He would be in Atlanta soon, so we arranged to meet in person.

The first meeting went well, and we were able to negotiate significant savings for the PGA Tour, which would increase further as a result of follow-up telephone discussions. That savings, along with some sponsorship commitments from Palmer & Cay, resulted in our appointment as Broker of Record for the PGA Tour. Against all odds, we had done it! This was a really big deal, taking a high-profile account from Marsh. One would think the new executives, all of whom were ex-Marsh, would be ecstatic. I did hear congratulations from Jim Meathe, but that was the end of it. I never heard a word from the national sales manager, Bill Lenhart. I soon found out that would be standard operating procedure for the young manager.

What was becoming evident in the new Palmer & Cay was that nothing the legacy offices or employees accomplished mattered. We were invisible. On the other hand, when Bill Failor, a producer who had moved down from Ohio, brought in a large account located back in Ohio, all the new guys were scrambling to take credit. Each one you talked with referred to the new account he sold. At first I thought they were bringing in a lot of new business, and then I realized they were all talking about the same account. I had seen this behavior before at prior companies, but it was usually a salesman repeating the same sales story in different ways to trick you into believing he was having a good year. As a group, these guys were taking it to a new level, each claiming the account as their own even if all they contributed was putting presentation binders together.

The real shame of the PGA Tour story is that the national sales manager was not the overachiever that we all anticipated. We never took advantage of the advertising opportunity in front of us as the official insurance broker of the PGA Tour. It never made it on our stationery or any of our advertising. Bill never grasped the professional opportunity for him personally to be part of the PGA Tour Program. What a waste. I'm not sure what the national sales manager was doing, but it wasn't working with the people producing business. We never heard from him—he didn't return phone calls or e-mails—but he could always tell you every day where to find Jim Meathe. I later learned that there was some kind of family connection between the Meathes and the Lenharts. For all I knew, Bill may have been working without a job description other than carrying Jim Meathe's briefcase.

As for me and my staff, we were committed to attend eight tournaments a year to be available to the golfers and their families. I immediately rolled up my sleeves and threw myself into the project by heading straight to Pebble Beach in California. Funny thing, the Pro-Am is not an official PGA Tour event, but well worth the trip.

Chapter 11

The Benefits Division

The natural separation within most insurance-brokerage firms is between commercial insurance and employee benefits. Commercial insurance pertains to most anything tied to tangible assets and to liabilities. Assets include automobiles, buildings, airplanes, inventory, machinery, and so on. Liabilities are basically anything for which you can get sued. While workmen's compensation has to do with employees, it has always been lumped into commercial insurance. Commercial insurance typically represents anywhere from 60 percent to 80 percent of most insurance-brokerage firms' business.

The remaining 20 percent to 40 percent usually falls into employee benefits. The services referred to as "benefits" almost always include health and welfare, which, generally speaking, is group insurance. Retirement services and/or actuarial services, where available, can make up a large component of the benefits department. Other benefits services can include human-resource consulting, payroll-deducted voluntary benefits, and sometimes investment services, which have special rules and regulations.

Within Palmer & Cay, benefits represented a significant contribution to total revenue. At the time, there were around fourteen offices with benefits departments, half of which existed before the Slabaugh, Morgan, and White acquisition. As part of the negotiations to sell their company, Ray Slabaugh and Dave Morgan were made codivision leaders of the Benefits Division. They tried to keep the name "Slabaugh Morgan" for the division, much like William Mercer Company, the benefits side of Marsh. John Cay would not hear of it.

My first exposure to Ray and Dave was several years back in a get-to-know-you dinner held in a private club for a few leaders of the Benefits Division. This dinner was in anticipation of Palmer & Cay buying their firm, Slabaugh, Morgan, and White. There were probably eight people in the room on that rainy night when Ray came over and said, "Ron, good to see you again," all the while smiling from ear to ear. I had no idea what he was talking about and shrugged my shoulders, holding my hands palms up. By now the rest of the room turned toward us. Ray continued, "It was in Jacksonville last year at your sales meeting. I was one of the speakers."

Now I was on the spot, knowing my answer would be embarrassing for Ray as he had assumed I was at that meeting. "Sorry Ray, I was not there last year because that was the week my son was born. I was probably at the hospital when you gave your talk." He was truly embarrassed, however, instead of saying "my bad," he insisted that he had met me and it must have been somewhere else. Everyone in the room knew he was just trying to save face.

Unfortunately for both of us, that encounter was the best our relationship was going to be. Every big company has a Ray—too bad at Palmer & Cay he ended up in my division. He didn't need problems with the manager of the largest office in his division, and I didn't need issues with someone who was technically my boss. Things could and would get much worse between us. This relationship was a departure from the years of positive and collaborative interaction I had with senior management, which had been a major joy of working at Palmer & Cay.

Actually, upon Lew's retirement, Bill Stanton was slated to be the head of the Benefits Division. Unfortunately, when John Cay, at the urging of Mike Crowley, struck the deal to buy Slabaugh, Morgan, and White, Ray and Dave were anointed codivision leaders as part of the selling agreement and Bill was pushed aside. In hindsight, it should have been the reverse.

When I joined Palmer & Cay, one of the things I embraced was the management style of John Cay and Lew Oden. They were all about what was best for the customers, the associates, and the company. Even after bringing in Mike Crowley as president, there were no obnoxious egos getting in the way. At first I had to do much of the work myself, including the mundane tasks like physically producing collated reports in presentation binders. All the while, I was bringing along Greg Waterstradt, the young producer hired on the same day that I signed on with the company. We worked well together, and he developed into an outstanding insurance broker. That became my operating procedure: hire good people, give them the tools for success, and provide guidance and support going forward. Like John and Lew before me, I found that hiring good people and stepping back to let them perform was the best way to succeed. Someone once asked me how I got my people to work so hard. The answer was simple: you put people in an environment with other top performers who are also working hard, and you have everyone trying their best.

Once in a budget presentation to managers, Mike Crowley, in going over compensation, pointed out, "The first manager to go over the salary budget will be Ron Collins. However, I know he will keep bringing the results to the bottom line, so it's okay." That is the kind of management support that makes a manager feel good about his job. Also, Palmer & Cay wanted realistic budget projections, not the "pie in the sky" plans you usually find with the big companies.

Unfortunately, Ray's style was typical old-time big-company, plus he felt that every thought that popped out of his head was original. I especially found it maddening that he always assumed everyone he hired was better than anyone else in the company at that position. As the head of our IT department said, "Ray thought his children were better looking than ours."

His partner Dave Morgan was the opposite, a calm, reasonable businessman. It was interesting that there were almost an even number of Palmer & Cay benefits offices as there were old Slabaugh, Morgan, and White offices. Most of the Palmer & Cay benefits offices made their budget and showed profits, while the others, for the most part, did not. The one exception was the Richmond office run by Julie White, a real professional.

When the company would not go along with Ray's plan to keep the Slabaugh, Morgan, and White name for the Benefits Division, he turned his attention to corporate titles. At the time, we used the usual officer's titles that most of corporate America adopted, starting with assistant vice president up to president and chairman. Ray, wanting to carve out a special niche, pushed for the Benefits Division to go with titles usually found in the consulting world, such as principals, partners, and managing partners. We even changed the name of the division to Palmer & Cay Consulting Group.

While our work was more akin to consulting than brokering, the consulting titles did not work in our organization. We went ahead and made the changes and put up with the consequences from then on out. The change in titles caused all kinds of confusion regarding where people fit in the hierarchy of the overall operation. People on the commercial side of the house won't bother to understand; they didn't know the difference between a managing partner and a mail sorter. You really can't blame the commercial side for the confusion, as they were the larger part of the organization. Eventually the Benefits Division would go with two titles. For example, my business card read Senior Vice President and Managing Partner.

Ray's view on consulting versus brokering explains why he said that I would be pleased with the changes in the company. Jim Meathe came from the world's largest broker, and Ray figured I would be glad that we were not turning into a consulting firm. It seemed to me that Ray felt that calling yourself a consultant made you special. The truth is that working as an hourly rate consultant is very limiting as far as producing revenue. There are only 2,080 hours in a work year that you can legitimately bill. My commission book of business usually exceeded $1 million per year. That comes out to $480 per hour for 2,080 hours, or over $600 per hour if you bill a more typical consulting time of 1,600 hours. Who is going to pay those kinds of rates for an insurance consultant? Over the years I had had a number of conversations with lawyers about billing hourly rates. The unscientific conclusion seemed to be that most lawyers would rather work on a project basis than on hourly rates. I had one lawyer tell me that charging by the hour "was like selling one brain cell at a time."

Chapter 12

The Atlanta Office

The main reception area for the Atlanta office was on the fourteenth floor, open to the elevator banks. Since Palmer & Cay had the whole floor, the doors were always wide open during business hours. The space was nicely appointed with a gold ship on the wall behind the receptionist desk. Incorporated in the space was a glassed-in conference room with "The Ship" logo etched in glass on each of the double doors. There was a boardroom-style table and heavy wood trim all around. It all looked nice, especially the view from the balcony. There was only one major drawback: never have a glassed-in conference room in the reception area. There was absolutely no privacy, which meant you could not meet with potential hires or acquisitions without the word getting around. Also, there was so much hall traffic that people in the conference room were always raising their heads to see who was walking through or reporting to the receptionist.

The offices on fourteen, in keeping with the Palmer & Cay culture, were not extravagant, not even those of the top executives. That's why red flags were raised when word got out that Jim Meathe wanted to refurbish the executive area. We already heard about what he did in Marsh's Chicago office. One day a designer from out of town showed up to take a look and get measurements. That alone was enough to set people off. Yet bringing in someone from Ohio when Palmer and Cay always did business with local people who had their insurance with us was almost more than people could take. Worst of all was when someone intercepted an incoming fax in the mailroom that was a drawing of Jim's new office—with a private restroom! People went nuts; that was so not our way. In fact, there was only one set of restrooms, male and female, for the whole floor of around sixty people.

The buzz about the private restroom eventually made it to Jim's attention. One day in a conversation we were having, he brought it up to me. "Can you believe people are upset and don't want me to have a restroom? After all, I am the president and work all kinds of hours and don't have time to always be walking down the hall."

All I could think of was how busy he had been the morning I caught him with his feet up on the desk, reading the newspaper. This obviously was all about ego. I was looking forward to hearing John's reaction.

My department was one floor down on the twelfth floor. Fourteen was actually the thirteenth floor, numbered fourteen to appease the superstitious. We occupied all of fourteen but only had about a third of the twelfth floor. However, being on twelve did provide a refuge from the chaos upstairs because the only people who came to see us had a purpose; there were no casual drop-in visits. In the months to come, I would grow to greatly appreciate this separate office arrangement.

Chapter 13

New Associates

One of my good friends once said, "Hiring an employee is like getting married after the first date. You never really know what you will get."

One of the hardest functions of management is hiring, or, as stated in the best business book ever, *Good to Great*, getting the right people on the right seats of the bus. Amazingly, this is the one thing that most people feel they would be good at if only they were in management. Over the years, I have tried to analyze this reaction and have concluded that people wrongly think hiring is instinctive, rather than an analytical process. People know what they like, and if they meet someone they approve of, either physically or socially, that approval carries far too much weight in forming their hiring opinions. Most people are not aware of how their personal preferences impact their view of others, therefore making it impossible to overcome their biases. A good manager has to be able to step back in sizing up a candidate, match the candidate for the open position, and clearly communicate expectations to the candidate. Even when the process is done correctly, there is still a good chance of failure because, in the end, human beings are all different. The best of managers will make hiring mistakes from time to time, usually when in a rush to fill a position, taking shortcuts, ending up with a less-than-ideal person for the job.

When hiring, I thought I was especially good at getting past my personal preferences or biases; however, John Cay was one of the best. A woman was once recommended to me as a potential producer. The day she showed up at my office, I was initially taken aback because she had bright, bleached-blond hair and wore rings on almost every finger, including her thumbs. In the interview, I realized there was something to this woman and decided to continue the hiring process. As part of that process, especially for producers, we always had someone on the senior-management team interview the candidates. Accordingly, I arranged for John Cay to meet with this somewhat-different salesperson. I was a little anxious to see his reaction, as he was a most conservative person. When we got together to discuss this candidate, to my surprise John said that once he got past the hair, he thought she would be a good producer for us. We went ahead and hired her and were proven right when she quickly put together a very productive book of business.

One day I received a call from Bill Stanton, my counterpart in the Washington, DC, office. Bill joined Palmer & Cay when we purchased several benefits offices from the accounting firm KPMG. Bill was a little older than me and had worked for a number of major firms over his career. He was a respected professional with an outstanding track record. We had only met a few years before, and we did not have the kind of relationship that included phone chitchat. So, when Bill called, I knew he had something on his mind.

"You seeing a lot of hiring in Atlanta?"

"Not for Atlanta, but a ton of people coming through for other offices. If they are in the benefits business I am usually asked to meet with them. Sometimes for salespeople also. Why, what's going on?"

"The new regional guy in DC is hiring a number of people, some of whom we had already looked at and rejected. And I hear they are all getting substantially more money for coming over."

"Well, I have had my doubts about some of those I have met. What do you think?"

"These people aren't going to be able to bring in business," he said. "We are just adding expenses."

From what I had already seen, Bill was right. There did not appear to be any process in place for staffing. If a candidate came from Marsh, they were hired without any analysis, peer review, or significant background check. It was as if Jim Meathe wanted to punish his former employer by taking away its people. Word was out on the street that the money was flowing at Palmer & Cay, and most of the new associates eagerly made the jump with little or no long-range thinking. This was particularly hard on me because I always agonized over every hire, no matter what the position. I grew up on the life insurance–company side of the business, where all salary-level employees went through extensive screening before being welcomed. For my first job out of school, I interviewed several times in Atlanta, twice in Portland, Maine, and finally a full day with an industrial psychologist. Before the process was over, I had been interviewed by every department head in the home office. Fourteen years later when I joined Palmer & Cay, I was required to fly down to Jacksonville, Florida, to meet with an outside psychologist. All this takes time and can be costly; however, hiring mistakes are considerably more expensive and can cause a great deal of damage to the organization. Thorough due diligence leads to a better hire and contributes to a more cohesive and cooperative team.

A word about industrial psychologists: I am a believer in the process for professional-level people for whom you are paying significant compensation. Psychologists are quick to point out that they cannot guarantee you a successful hire, but can more often than not help you avoid a sure failure. In saying that, I am reminded of a young man I interviewed at my former employer. This young man, let's call him Paul since I can't remember his name, made a presentable impression even though he showed up on crutches. His injury was the result of playing softball, which is usually the case in Atlanta when you see a younger guy wearing a business suit with his foot in a cast. Paul worked for an insurance company in the Midwest and was moving to Atlanta to be with his fiancée. He spoke elegantly about his family up-bringing, especially his love for his parents. He seemed to be such a good fit that I had my direct boss meet him with me in the room. That conversation went so well that my boss brought in the president of our company to speak with this remarkable potential account executive. Both executives wanted me to hire Paul on the spot.

After hearing this man's story for the third time, I became leery. He was sounding a little too practiced; always the exact same words in each telling. The wrath of senior management came down on me when I refused to hire this man until he met with our outside psychologist. Paul spent four hours with the psychologist. In keeping with my usual practice, I spoke by phone with the good doctor immediately after Paul's interview. The only surprise in our conversation was how adamant he was about me not hiring Paul. Psychologists usually don't say, "Absolutely do not hire." Except in the case of Paul. When I informed my boss and his boss, the president, that I would not be hiring Paul, it was as if I had stolen from the company. They were not happy. To make things worse, we soon found out Paul went to work for one of our competitors who had started his own company with business he took with him when he left our company.

Through people in different insurance companies, I kept my eye on Paul's situation. It didn't take long. Six months into his new life, Paul was fired from his job and his fiancée threw him out of the house when she caught him cheating on her. When I passed the news on to my senior management that we had dodged a bullet, I was not met with any satisfaction. Sadly, they were still mad that I went against their wishes by not hiring Paul. The lesson learned is that being right is not always a career enhancer.

The best managers and the best companies take the hiring process seriously for good reason. In today's litigious environment, problem or underperforming employees are hard to get rid of, and often the poisonous disharmony they create impedes the performance of the entire work unit. To use a sports analogy, in the early eighties, the year before the University of Georgia won the National Football Championship, there was dissension in the locker room, and the results showed. During the off-season, a number of troubled players left the program. Some left on their own volition, or because of academic ineligibility, and some were asked to leave. The next year the team came together with the help of a running back named Herschel Walker (my former client) and beat Notre Dame in the Sugar Bowl. Most coaches will tell you about the importance of team chemistry in the locker room. The same applies to business.

In looking back at all the hiring I was involved with, the story of the interns typifies the difference that a good selection can bring to a company. Each summer, the Atlanta office would hire several interns, usually from the Risk Management School at the University of Georgia. Even with all the commotion going on within Palmer & Cay, we chose to continue the intern program.

Unlike the other hirings, the intern program was really a very low-cost issue. Three young people were interviewed for two positions.

Because I was paying for part of the intern program out of my budget, I interviewed each candidate. All three were sharp college students; however, in my mind the one named Matt stood out as a must hire. In the interview, I found out to my surprise that I knew Matt's father from previous business dealings, which reinforced my opinion of him.

When I followed up with the producer in charge of the intern program that year, I learned that my candidate was not chosen for either of the two positions. I strolled down to Frank Beard's office (acting head of the Atlanta office) and voiced my opinion. Frank responded, "If you feel that strongly about the guy, go ahead and hire him. You are paying a third of the costs anyway."

The rest, as they say, is history. Matt distinguished himself that summer and was offered a job upon graduation. He almost got away from Palmer & Cay, as we were not the only ones to recognize his potential. His next position in the insurance business after Palmer & Cay was to move to another insurance broker for a short time before joining, as producer, an agency started by a former Palmer & Cay producer. Since then he has become one of the most successful commercial-insurance producers in Atlanta.

Of all the people I personally interviewed from Marsh, there was only one exception to the Marsh exit crowd. A young guy, whose name I have long forgotten, arrived at our reception area from the Northern Virginia/Washington, DC, area. He was a producer with Marsh specializing in commercial insurance for the high-tech industry clustered around the Beltway in DC. He had added approximately forty new accounts in an eighteen-month period. Needless to say, everyone wanted this whiz kid to join Palmer & Cay. Right after lunch, he was sent down to my office for a quick half-hour interview. He was as sharp as billed and had a real grasp of the situation. When I asked him how he was so successful in such a short period of time, his response was that he worked for the world's largest broker and happened into the high-tech industry as it was developing in the DC area. Unlike all the others, he knew where the business came from and how well he had it at Marsh. Also, he was too young to have been part of the Jim Meathe worship faction. He could not be bribed with promises of money or position. Right then, I knew he would not be switching companies to take a flyer with tiny, little Palmer & Cay.

Chapter 14

New Executive Syndrome

As outside advisors, insurance brokers, while working with corporate clients, experience every variety of executives and their approaches to the decision process. Most executives feel, naturally so, that they should have an impact on the organization they have been hired to manage, or at least their particular area. A good executive will come into an organization, look around, and take measure of what is there before trying to transform the business model. Others just come in and blow things up, thinking they know better than the people who came before them. These executives push out the people with the institutional memory. They never really understand the heart and soul of an organization and often move on after making a mess of things.

An indication of things to come may have been in the form of a photograph of the new board. The picture, which started showing up on the desks of the board members, was in a frame that had one word embedded: "Imagine." This was the kind of thing you could purchase at the business-motivation store at the mall where they also sell framed posters with phrases designed to inspire. I remember thinking the group in the picture did not look especially eager to work together. When I asked John Cay about the picture, his response was "Oh, that is something Jim did." I did not sense any particular support for the sentiment.

There were two issues in which I was personally involved that would set the tone in my mind about the new organization. First, I assumed that if this new president was the sharp, hard-driving executive that he was billed to be, he would come to certain conclusions about the performance, or lack thereof, in the Benefits Division. This would help me immensely, as I was through dealing with Ray. In fact, Lew had set things up so that I didn't really report to Ray, but with Lew retired, Ray was trying to exert more influence over my operation. Shortly after all the off-site meetings started, I had the chance to have a conversation with Ray. In that conversation, Ray shared with me that his partner, Dave, had almost left the firm due to all the heat he and Ray were taking at board meetings for the underperformance of the Benefits Division. The rhetoric had escalated since most of the offices dragging down our division were old Slabaugh, Morgan, and White offices. Early on, John Cay wisely decided not to let them comingle the books to hide the lack of results. Of the two, Dave took things deeply personally, while criticism just rolled off Ray's back.

Since this was still before Jim Meathe moved to Atlanta, Ray invited himself to Chicago so that he and Dave could spend the day going over their plans for the Benefits Division. To my surprise, Dave told me that it was a great visit and Jim was very supportive of their efforts. As Dave was telling me about the visit to Chicago, I thought, *How could this be? Surely Jim must know how to read financial statements.* It would not take long to figure this out; Jim Meathe was very susceptible to people who agreed with him, especially if he felt they would change their loyalties from John Cay. In this case, he had read Ray correctly, as events later would confirm. And now I was stuck with an emboldened Ray Slabaugh.

The second issue I was dealing with was the joint venture with the law firm Troutman Sanders. I was starting to get word that Jim did not approve. Because he had not talked with me about it, I assumed that he just did not understand the potential for new business. When we finally sat down to discuss the situation, he informed me that he was bringing on a few guys in Michigan to start a TPA firm and the joint venture would be a direct conflict with that effort. TPAs adjudicate health claims mostly for self-funded group-insurance programs. It is an intricate, complicated process, mostly performed on computer terminals by relatively lower-paid workers. For fourteen years I had fought to keep Palmer & Cay out of this business, even when one was offered to John Cay at no charge. From my past experience running a TPA for a national firm, I knew it was a people-intensive, low-margin business fraught with lawsuits. My previous employer ended up divesting their national TPA at a significant loss, mostly to get away from all the litigation. This being said, I did not use this argument with Jim, as I did not want to be labeled a naysayer on one of his first initiatives. Instead, I just pointed out that the joint venture was not in conflict with the TPA effort and it might even help develop new business for the TPA. Jim dug his heels in and went apoplectic when I told him, "Too late, we have a signed contract."

I would later learn that these guys Jim was supporting had already bankrupted one TPA and had a propensity to close down at noon on Fridays in favor of liquid lunches. When we were appointed on the PGA Tour account, the Michigan group tried to convince me to place the business with them. Even Jim would not risk such a prestigious account in their hands.

As a result of Jim's opposition to the joint venture, a meeting was set up in the Midtown offices of Troutman Sanders to talk things out. Unfortunately, John Cay was going to be out of town, meaning it would be just Jim and me. In the car on the way to the meeting, one of Jim's people tried to remind him of his noncompete-contract status with Marsh, and that he should not have hugged the woman from Minnesota that was in our offices that morning to talk about joining Palmer & Cay. Any contact with active Marsh employees could be interpreted as a violation, especially if they had traveled from another city to Atlanta. Everyone was working really hard at keeping Jim away from any possible appearances of impropriety. His response was that no piece of paper was going to stop him from giving anyone a hug and kiss. He then turned his attention to me and started railing about John signing the joint-venture agreement, which, like most contracts, was written on paper.

Although the joint venture was the brainchild of my friend Travis DeHaven, who was also in attendance, the meeting was actually hosted by the managing partner, Bob Webb. Bob had been a litigator before taking over the management of the firm at an incredibly young age. As you might expect, the scene was fairly intimidating. The conference room with twelve-foot ceilings, long marble table, high-end leather chairs, mahogany walls, and a blue-suited, white-shirted litigator drilling down with questions could make a person pause. In that environment, Jim Meathe would offer no good reason for his opposition to the joint venture, instead refusing to say in person that he definitely would or would not move forward. In the end, it was agreed we would continue the discussion at a later date. I knew then that this would not end well.

The next time John Cay was in Atlanta, he called me into his office to hear about the meeting. When I told John that Jim did everything he could to derail the project, a concerned look came over his face. I then mentioned, "The thing I don't get is why Jim is going out of his way to piss off one of the major law firms in the city when he is trying to get into a country club. You know they will have members of every club in town. Good luck with that!"

A genuine smile came across John's face. "Yeah, that's right."

The one club that Jim had a chance to get into was one of the clubs to which Joe Rogers (head of Waffle House Corporate) was a member. After months of waiting, Jim's membership was eventually rejected, but not because of any lawyer. I would later learn from a member that it was a Marsh sales guy of questionable reputation who voted Jim down. How fitting, done in by one of his own.

In many conversations with Jim, I tried to convince him to bless the joint venture. I could not believe he would not support such a considered program, one to which we had devoted so much planning time. Unfortunately, Jim refused to budge and John Cay, after initially saying we would go ahead, would not step in to overrule him. While I was still reeling from the turn of events with John's reluctance to get involved, word got back to me that Jim had gone to the board, and they pressured John to step aside to let Jim have his way. At this time it was hard to conclude that the board knew what was going on. Something this important should have been questioned, and Jim should have had to defend his position. Yet, they just sat back and let Jim rule as he desired with no accountability. This was the first time I had a real sense of how serious our predicament was becoming. Prior to this time, John Cay would never have allowed himself to be publicly embarrassed by someone at Palmer & Cay overriding one of his decisions. And believe me, I heard about it from the lawyers at Troutman Sanders, many of whom said, "Who's running Palmer & Cay?" This whole episode was so unlike John that I began to wonder about his actions and, for the first time, worry about the future of the company.

There was one more meeting at Troutman Sanders, which Jim attended by phone while I sat there in person by myself to face the music. It was obvious that Jim would not let the joint venture move forward, and Bob Webb was not happy. Afterward, the lawyer who was to be the head of the joint venture presented a demand letter to John Cay for $275,000 for the time he delayed his career while we sorted things out. John ended up paying him. I would hear about the joint venture one more time later in the year when Dave Morgan told me that Jim Meathe docked my bonus by $8,000 because he did not approve of my handling of the project. Great, he cost the company a quarter of a million in direct cost, plus the lost man-hours over two years, and I am the one who had to pay. Jim actually brought up the subject of my bonus in a food line during a company function where he knew I could not respond. He was in front of me in the line set up in the main conference room for some special event. He turned to me and quickly mentioned that he had to dock my bonus because of the way I handled the joint venture. That put me in the position of either causing a scene or keeping quiet. I said nothing. By that time, I was sure he would not last at the company and my payback would be smiling at him as he left for the last time.

So, what was the real story about the joint venture? I can only conclude that Jim was afraid that it would be successful and he would have no ownership from a management prospective. Maybe I made a mistake in billing it as a game changer; however, Travis and I would be proven right several years later when a number of major firms became very successful with similar business plans.

By now, John Cay's abdication of leadership had become most troubling. None of us had seen this situation before. When it came to company money, John was always very aggressive. Not long ago, Palmer & Cay put $250,000 into a business deal that went south, losing all our initial investment. Our partners in that venture became lackadaisical about the outcome, acting like it was no big deal. John called for a meeting with the principals and threatened to sue each one personally. That situation was resolved with Palmer & Cay receiving insurance commissions to make up for the loss. John was willing to fight for our money in that case, which was insignificant in comparison to what the company was currently experiencing.

Chapter 15

The Partnership

Word started getting out that Jim and the board were going to change the ownership composition and structure of the company. The idea was to change from a privately held stock company to a partnership arrangement similar to law firms and accounting firms. There were several problems with this idea: first, John Cay was not about to give up controlling ownership of his company; and second, over 40 percent of the company was owned by employees who had laid out cold, hard cash to buy shares. It would be difficult—if not impossible—to issue and sell new shares without diluting the values for the existing shareholders. My biggest concern was that the company might start issuing stock options. Having seen stock options at other places, I knew how subjective and arbitrary the option awards could get. Plus, stock options aren't free; they cost the issuing company significantly.

Outside consultants were brought in to figure out how to accomplish the changeover. At the same time, it was getting close to the annual valuation performed by a company that specialized in valuing insurance brokers and agencies. Targeting the new stock price would be difficult due to all the expenses associated with the new offices and people who had not yet earned any revenue for the company.

While this was going on, I became reacquainted with Dick Fortier of the Teren Group. The Teren Group was a management-consulting company founded by Dick's father, Ren Fortier. Ren had been one of General Eisenhower's staff officers in World War II and parlayed that experience into a consulting business. Frank Beard had brought Dick into Palmer & Cay to help our firm. Dick and I had breakfast one morning to catch up from the days we met at my former employer thirteen years earlier. He was already aware of the changes at Palmer & Cay and was very encouraging about the future. According to Dick, he had seen this type of change before and if done right, the value created by a partnership could be very rewarding financially. I walked away from that breakfast feeling better about what was happening. Though I may not have liked all the changes to the company, I was not against a large enhancement of my wealth.

Another conversation that I found encouraging was with Ian Robb, the head of our human-resources department. Ian was one of the few ex-Marsh people who was hired at Palmer & Cay prior to the invasion brought on by Jim Meathe. Ian was a survivor of 9/11, having worked in one of the Twin Towers in New York City. On the morning of September 11, 2001, Ian was actually on an elevator when the airplanes struck. He was able to get off at a lower floor and leave the scene. Although his Palmer & Cay office was in Savannah, he was constantly in and out of Atlanta. It was on one of those visits that he and I had occasion to discuss the new organization. Knowing that he was nearing the end of his working career, Ian understood he would not be around to benefit from the partnership arrangement. Even so, he spoke wistfully about the possibilities that such an opportunity could provide. I had a great deal of respect for Ian and his words carried weight with me.

The consultants presented the general approach of the plan at the company sales conference in September on Hilton Head Island, South Carolina. The conference attendees represented most of the current shareholders, plus most of those who would be given an opportunity to become shareholders. While the concept was intriguing to contemplate, the consultants were short on details. The one troubling thing in my mind was that the valuation company seemed to qualify everything they said with noncommittal terms. It was as if they didn't really believe it themselves. After the presentation, I tried to pin down the presenter one on one, and he seemed very uncomfortable. It was like he had been told what to say and could say no more. Getting him to open up was like trying to stab a marble with a steak knife.

Eventually, a plan with details would be announced with implementation sometime the following year. There would be four levels of partners who would be required to have a minimum ownership. Even though we were moving to partnership nomenclature, for legal reasons Palmer & Cay would still be a stock company. For example, as a senior vice president I would become a managing partner and be required to buy in at that level in order to retain that position. Since my ownership already exceeded the minimum for my position, I might be forced to sell some shares back to the company if it turned out there were not enough shares for the new people. Needless to say, many of the legacy Palmer & Cay people were not happy, and most of the new people were excited, scrambling to find a way to raise the money they would need to buy in.

Soon lists were being circulated with names of potential partners. I was given a list of names for my four subsets: Health and Welfare, Actuarial, Human-Resource Consulting, and Palmer & Cay Investments. The list must have come from the HR department because it was fairly well done with few exceptions. I was given a time slot for a meeting with Jim Meathe to review my list, because he was personally checking every name. In our meeting, as I was about to question him on who would be making the value judgments for the rest of the company, he jumped all over me. "I don't want to hear any of that talk. We will make the best decisions possible. Besides, when it is all over not everyone may be getting partnerships. For example, you may not even be on the final list."

As I was taking notes on my list, I could see him looking for my reaction out of the corner of his eye and responded, "Well good, Jim, that will save me thousands of dollars."

He knew he hadn't pushed any buttons with me and started to laugh, telling me to get out of his office. I suspected that in spite of some of the issues that had transpired, he liked me, a suspicion that was later confirmed by other executives from statements that Jim shared with them. I was not one of the yes-men who slobbered all over him, and I ran the biggest and most profitable benefits office in the system.

One other thing that worried me about this change in title nomenclature was how companies often used this type of changeover as a way of shuffling the hierarchy when they know the decisions are controversial. One of my former employers wanted to promote some people at one level but not all of them, so they made some of the senior vice presidents into executive vice presidents and one senior vice president became senior executive vice president. How silly; as if people won't see through that ruse. Plus, how pretentious is a business card with "senior executive vice president" on it for an office with only two hundred employees. Very embarrassing!

Chapter 16

Shortcuts to Success

The Jim Meathe strategy for building the company was pretty simple. From people in our accounting department who prepared illustrations for capital-raising meetings, we confirmed what we already knew about the strategy. In those meetings and in overheard phone conversations, Jim would articulate his approach. The plan was to raid talent from other companies, particularly Marsh and Aon (second-largest national insurance brokerage firm), and expect those people to bring their business with them. That way Palmer & Cay would avoid the traditional business-acquisition costs except for the additional salary expense for the people coming on board. We would not be paying the salaries and expenses while waiting for producers to gain traction and develop business from scratch. If it worked, this would be infinitely more profitable — or so the management party line went.

There were a couple of problems with this novel idea. First, from a moral standpoint, was this approach ethical? In insurance brokerage, as in accounting and law, it is accepted that individuals from time to time choose to change firms, and they may or may not be able to take their accounts with them. The same goes for taking their staffs or key employees. As long as it is onesie-twosies, no problem. But what we were talking about here was a wholesale raid, especially in the Midwest offices of Marsh. How does a company protect itself from the same threat if it behaves in this manner? Virtually every professional employee at the major firms had noncompete contracts. When hiring producers at Palmer & Cay, we never asked a new associate to break their contract. What were we expecting from all these new people?

The second problem can be summed up in the words of a former Palmer & Cay manager: "Never poke a large dog with a sharp stick!" Did anyone ever consider that we were a tiny, little company with $135 million in revenue compared to the multibillion-dollar behemoth Marsh? As should have been anticipated, Marsh did not take this well, and to top things off Jim Meathe proceeded to sue Marsh to get out of his existing contract that restricted his activities. What was he thinking? Before it was all over, we would be in litigation in every state we operated in, our legal fees growing to over $250,000 per month. The annual cost for defending ourselves on this single issue was almost $3 million, or approximately 2.14 percent of annual revenue. This was unheard of in our industry. Once again, we were charting into dangerous, unprecedented waters.

For our little firm, those legal costs were real money. On top of the money issue, I was not sure there was any benefit to the company in getting Jim out of his Marsh contract. We had enough senior people to deal with whatever issues came our way. After many months of bleeding legal fees, we sent our former president Mike Crowley to New York to settle things with Marsh. While he was in the headquarters of Marsh, he ran into Jeff Greenberg, the chairman/CEO of Marsh and son of the legendary Hank Greenberg of AIG. When Mike complemented Jeff on his organization, the reply from Greenberg was "I once felt the same way about Palmer & Cay." Our pristine reputation had taken a big hit. Not a good sign.

Mike's meeting was with Bill Choate, who managed a large part of Marsh out of Charlotte, North Carolina. When Mike asked what it would take to settle this dispute, Bill responded, "Fifty million dollars." They were essentially asking for a third of our company! When Mike recovered his speech, he asked how Marsh came up with that number, since we had not taken anywhere near that amount of business from Marsh. Choate's answer was "That is just what the company allocated to this problem, and you need to know that is not even a quarterly rounding error for Marsh."

When you think about it, Jim was betting the whole company on his assumption that the plan would work. He was risking everything on his first big bet. I am reminded of how a friend described the consequences of making any decision. Three things can happen: (1) The decision was right and the plan worked, so all is well; (2) the plan only partially worked and there was a waste of time, energy, and money; or (3) the plan failed and all that was at risk is lost. Jim's decision to go all in and to accumulate so much debt put the entire company at risk. It was an all-or-nothing proposition. I wondered if any thought was given to trying this new approach in one area or location as a test. Would that have been too much like a real business plan?

An example of how bad executive decisions can have a negative impact on a company can be seen in a real-life situation for one of our former clients in the Midwest. This company had made shopping carts for years. They would manufacture and assemble the carts all year and take orders during a brief selling season once a year. Palmer & Cay provided the group insurance for the employees and their families. The company was bought out by a private-equity firm. The private-equity firm brought in a big-name national consulting firm to provide their MBA-driven financial-analysis recommendations. When they started implementing the changes, the gray-haired, old gentleman who ran the place decided that it would be a good time to retire since he was not in agreement with management. They let him get out the door before a suitable replacement could be found or trained. Following the advice of the consultants, the company made two critical decisions. First, they decided to build the carts to order instead of building them all year and storing them until shipment. The second decision was to outsource the manufacturing of the wheels instead of keeping the work in house.

You can guess what happened. In the first year of this new approach, there was a problem with the wheels from the supplier. When the orders came in, the carts could not be completed and delivered. The company missed a whole selling season and lost the loyalty of their longtime customers. The company did not survive the second year, the equity firm lost their investment, and in these situations the employees are harmed even if there is a reorganization in bankruptcy. Of course, the consultants were well paid before they disappeared. The sea of business is full of these stories, and there seems to be a never-ending list of navigation mistakes people can make with severe consequences. I was beginning to realize Palmer & Cay was entering those waters.

Chapter 17

The Big Walkout

While driving down Peachtree Street one day, I received a phone call informing me that Karen Lehman was leaving the company. Karen, our CFO, was one of my favorite people. I really respected her work ethic and her willingness to cooperate with those of us in the field offices. Immediately, I pulled over into a parking lot and called Karen's office. Even though we really did not have a close personal relationship, that call proved to be very intimate. As she told me about the abuse and profanity she endured, she began to cry and I felt awful. Jim Meathe was so determined to get his own CFO, one loyal to him, that he made her life miserable. He would ask her to change formats on reports and then criticize her for the outcomes. And the language he used was atrocious. I could not believe the prim and proper John Cay would allow this in his company; after all, he never swore. This was only one of the many times that John would disappoint me and all the loyal followers of the company.

Still in disbelief, I talked with John's secretary by phone, and she confirmed the bad language and behavior. I asked Monica, "What does John say about the cursing?"

"He called Jim in to explain that was not the Palmer & Cay way and asked him to treat people with respect, but it didn't do any good."

I could not believe Jim wasn't fired on the spot. I guess by then John was in too deep with the new board members.

A search began to replace Karen, one of the few positions that did not go straight to a Marsh employee. After months of waiting, we finally hired someone whom no one knew and who would work out of both Savannah and Atlanta. This certainly would give Jim Meathe control of the financial data. I wasn't sure how this was an improvement, since when Karen walked out the door so much of our institutional memory walked out with her, complicating things for everyone.

Soon after Karen left, an introductory meeting for the Atlanta office was held in a conference room of a nearby hotel. Everyone in the Atlanta office was invited, including employees of all levels and any out-of-town employees who happened to be around. Gus Gussenhoven and Joe Platt were asked to say a few words about their relationship with Palmer & Cay as new board members. Gus went first and explained how close he and Joe were, going back to their J&H days before being purchased by Marsh. Then he pivoted to how he helped another employee tie a bow tie for a tuxedo, and finally spoke about flying his own jet and how his wife didn't want him to pilot by himself anymore due to his age.

When Gus gave up the stage to Joe, we were regaled with tales of Joe's recent exotic travels. Dead silence from the crowd; the working class was not into it! Frank Beard, sensing the mood of the group, got up and made a joke about spending the weekend with his grandchildren. No one laughed. In the end, their insufferable egos had them talking to themselves.

For some reason Ray Slabaugh was in attendance, and when one of the speakers announced a new initiative for employee education, Ray raised his hand and told the room, "The Benefits Division already has a chief learning officer. In fact, we have two CLOs."

Doug Hutcherson, sitting off to the side a few rows away, slightly turned and looked right at me to make eye contact. Doug had been extremely critical of the changes in the company, and this talk of superfluous hiring was more than he could stomach. The look on his face was pure rage; he was livid. If anything, the get-to-know-you meeting was an unmitigated disaster. How could these people be so tone deaf? The answer is quite simple: the new board members, our new president, and many of their followers came from large, bureaucratic organizations where they were not the founders, nor the intellectual force behind the organization, nor the visionaries who made things happen. They were just people who could work within the system that someone else devised.

As a broker who worked with many organizations and executives in my career, I have often witnessed the failures of people who left the comfort of the big companies, mistaking their rise in the organization for individual talent, only to wake up to the harsh reality that they really were not the instigator of corporate success. I was once asked to provide insurance for a start-up company owned by a former senior officer of a major industrial company out of Chicago. This man married a wealthy woman from Atlanta and decided to live in Atlanta but build his new plant in Kentucky. After he went through all the money he saved from his corporate career and all of his new wife's money, he drove his car into the backyard of his stylish, uptown Buckhead home and put a gun in his mouth. The bottom line of the story is that just because you held a high title in a large organization doesn't necessarily translate to being a star executive in an entrepreneurial setting.

In September, a bombshell hit the Atlanta office. I was in my office when word came down that a group of people on fourteen had walked out together. I scrambled upstairs and started around the floor. Doug Hutcherson was not in his office, but his personal items were still there. When I turned around to the workstations of his staff, they were all empty, cleaned out. Down the hall, John Varner's office was cleaned out, his assistant still in place. Farther down the hall, Philip Holly's office and staff were all gone. By the time I worked my way back to the reception area, Fran Millar was standing there with a few other people. When he saw me coming, he laughingly said, "Look, Ron is wondering, 'Where did everyone go?'"

That day we lost a total of twelve sales and support people who represented around 15 percent of the commercial side of the office. In addition to losing several key salespeople, just to stick it to the company, they walked out with the receptionist and the mailroom person without giving notice. This group would become the nucleus of the Lockton Company's Atlanta office, one of our rivals trying to get a foothold in the Atlanta market. Lockton was the only privately held broker in the country larger than Palmer & Cay.

A meeting was called for the next day in the main reception area of the Atlanta office. Frank Beard addressed the crowd, calling for calm and asking people to say little to outsiders other than that these people had left. Will Underwood, one of the producers, addressed the group and proclaimed he was the first one contacted by Lockton and he decided to stay at Palmer & Cay. I'm not sure why he thought he should get credit for his announcement, because he obviously hadn't warned management of what he knew was about to happen. How was that reassuring to the troops? The looks on people's faces told the real story: things were taking a turn for the worse.

Looking back, I should have anticipated that we would lose some salespeople. First, in recent meetings Jim Meathe had announced to the producers that he was going to change the compensation arrangement. The producers rightly figured that it would be a less lucrative Marsh-lookalike program. In fact a number of them, especially Philip Holly, had mentioned that to me. Second, studies of corporate change indicate that in times of upheaval it is the top performers who leave first. They have the confidence and desire to move on from a deteriorating situation to what they perceive will be a better one.

Losing Doug Hutcherson posed more than just a perception problem for the Atlanta office; it caused real financial concerns. Doug had one of the biggest blocks of business, including one of the largest accounts in the company. He was very close to his clients, and it was probable that they would follow him out the door. Just when we needed to be adding significant new business, we were about to lose, on the basis of anticipated compensation changes, a good chunk that took years to obtain. For me, there was a personal angle to this story.

It started several years earlier when I was a guest of my good friend Fred Schremp at the TPC Golf Tournament in Florida. I had met Fred many years before, and his wife worked for me when they married. As we walked along the fairways following Phil Mickelson on that sunny day, Fred explained that he had been calling on his West Point classmates prospecting for new business. Many former West Pointers of his age who left the military were now owners of companies or senior executives. One of the larger companies was CKE (which owned several fast-food chains, including Carl's Jr. and Hardee's), where both the CEO and CFO were graduates of the US Military Academy. Fred, like me, was a benefits specialist; however, CKE's needs were in the property/casualty area. He had gone up to New York to negotiate directly with AIG but was having a difficult time. I explained that AIG was one of the toughest companies to work with and he needed a partner he could trust to help him. Naturally, I suggested Palmer & Cay.

A meeting was set up for Fred to meet Doug Hutcherson, which led to more meetings and numerous trips to California to establish a relationship with CKE. There was even a hunting and golf trip by CKE executives to Savannah to stay at John Cay's plantation. After a lengthy courtship, a deal was struck from which, even after splits to both Fred's company and an in-house broker of CKE, there would be a very healthy commission for Palmer & Cay.

So now, instead of the quick, cheap addition of income called for in the Meathe plan, we were losing large, hard-fought-for business that took several years to develop. And the whole insurance industry knew about it. John Cay asked if I would call Fred to see what he could do to help us save the CKE account. I knew what the answer would be, but was obligated to place a halfhearted call to Fred. Fred recognized my participation in initiating the relationship; however, he made it clear it was too late to intervene since Doug had built a solid relationship with CKE that was now beyond Fred's control.

Chapter 18

Results, or Lack of Results

One of the things that differentiates the small, privately held firm from the giant, national, publicly traded company is the sharing of financial information. Public companies have certain governmental restrictions on when they may or when they must release financial information. As a privately held company, Palmer & Cay was not subject to those requirements. From day one at Palmer & Cay, there was a monthly report that listed every work group (known as profit centers) by location, providing monthly and year-to-date numbers. The numbers included revenue, expenses, and pretax profits. Actual numbers for the current year were compared to the business plan for the same year and the actual results for the prior year. For managers, there was no place to hide. All the other managers and senior management knew exactly how their group was doing. Everyone was accountable. Some small firms even publish a list of every producer (salespeople) in descending order based on monthly and year-to-date sales. One company with multiple offices actually televises the list of producers to each office so every employee can see how sales are progressing.

Large companies provide most of the same information; however, due to their sheer size, the information is often rolled up into larger categories or divisions. There are just more places to hide in large organizations. Another trick of large companies is to change the reporting format to hide weaknesses or underachievers. We were to get to that soon enough at Palmer & Cay.

For the first few months, no one expected the reports to reflect the activities of the new people. However, at the six-month mark we all started watching the monthly reports for signs of growth. In the insurance-brokerage business, a client can change brokers with the stroke of a pen, and Jim's plan depended on many companies doing just that. As the months rolled by, there was almost no new business, and the monthly profit-center reports became agonizingly embarrassing for the new regime. Most of the Midwest offices had zeros where the revenue should have been and alarmingly growing numbers on the expense side. Obviously, the pretax-revenue numbers were all negatives under these circumstances.

So, what was going wrong with the business plan that was presented to all the stakeholders, especially the bankers? One only needs to pick up a copy of *Good to Great* and reread the part about getting the right people in the right seats on the bus. Almost all of the new people hired from Marsh came from the management level. The problem was that the large national firms had focused efforts on institutionalizing their business by assigning multiple people to each account with emphasis on the larger accounts. That way, once an account was on board, the salespeople moved onto other opportunities, and after time no one person controlled the account. Management became scorekeepers with no control on the business.

When I saw names like Motorola on the prospect list, I knew we were in trouble. Yes, we had more than our share of large, some nationally known, accounts; however, we worked very hard to obtain those accounts, and they did not flock to us just because a salesperson changed firms. The one thing that most of the new people got wrong was that when at Marsh or Aon, the customer was buying the services and systems made available by these large brokerage firms and not necessarily the individual talents of any specific person. At Palmer & Cay, we were selling the hands-on approach of a boutique firm. With Palmer & Cay, the customer was getting the close attention of senior, experienced advisors. These are two entirely different value propositions.

In a one-on-one meeting with Jim, we were discussing a consultant that I was recruiting. My issue was that I was uncomfortable with the income this individual wanted. Jim's response was to go ahead and hire him and then go out and find a couple of $100,000 accounts. That was the mentality of these former Marsh people. If I had known where to find two new $100,000 accounts, I would not have been sitting there with him. At the end of the meeting I asked Jim what would happen if his plans for the company did not work out. His response: "It's going to work, Ron. I would not be bringing in all my friends if it wasn't going to work."

That reminds me of another nifty little maneuver going on about projections. Potential sales estimates were being based on percentages of business in the sales pipeline with the assumption that those were real prospects on the list submitted from each office. That technique only works when there is a history to base it on. Okay for the old Palmer & Cay, not so good for the new producers. The projections were a myth, yet everything was being based on those numbers. Production doesn't happen just because you project it on a piece of paper; there must be a realistic basis for the numbers. Those of us who were old hands at Palmer & Cay could see what was happening.

Chapter 19

Bonus Double Cross

While all the changes were going on companywide, I had a difficult issue—not of my own making—within my main revenue driver, the Health and Welfare Group. This group represented half of the forty-plus people in my area of responsibility, but accounted for over 75 percent of the revenue and, in some years, over 50 percent of the total bottom line of the entire Atlanta office. The group consisted of nine producers (including myself), twelve account executives and account managers, and three administrative people. We were clearly the number-one benefits operation in the company.

One evening several years back, riding in a car on the way to a restaurant with Lew Oden and Ray Slabaugh, the success of this group became the topic of discussion. Ray turned to me in the back seat and, in an almost accusatory tone, said, "You *should* be successful—you have all the horses." He spoke as if I was lucky to have them, totally discounting all the years of hard work building a first-class operation while generating the revenue to support it all.

I replied, "Yeah, I know, Ray. Where do you think those people came from? I selected them on purpose. Our success is no accident." As Ray turned around with his face all wrinkled up, I looked over to see Lew chuckling at our exchange.

This story is so indicative of Ray's mentality. In his mind, I didn't deserve credit for the years of hard work, thousands of hours creating revenue, and anguish-filled nights thinking about hiring decisions. In Ray's world, there was no history before he showed up on the scene. According to him, I was just lucky to have "the horses."

The purpose of telling the story of that conversation is to set the stage for what had been developing for the last year. The year before, Ray and Dave, working out of the Richmond, Virginia, office, decided the company needed a new incentive program for the people in the Benefits Division. They put together a program with certain criteria that, if met, would trigger bonuses for the successful offices. I'm not sure if they came up with this approach using internal resources or if they went to outside consultants. Anyway, after getting board approval, the program was disseminated to all the benefits offices in writing for distribution to the associates. It did not take long for my group of overachievers to figure out they had a real chance to boost their income. For the next twelve months, the bonus program became a constant focus of discussion within the Health and Welfare Group. Each month when the financials came out, I could count on a group of people standing in front of my desk, asking where we stood.

My problem was that I felt like I was living a lie. I never really believed that the bonuses would be paid. The reason I felt that way is that I had watched John Cay kind of but not really agree to other arrangements. I had seen him listen to Ray like a distracted husband listens to his wife and nod in agreement, only to later find out she scheduled their daughter's wedding on Masters weekend or the annual kickoff of her garden club at their house on Super Bowl Sunday. I kept asking Ray, "Are you sure about this?" To which he would answer, "Yes, John was in on the discussions. He knows all about it."

Well, you can guess what happened. At the end of our fiscal year (June 30), the company as a whole was feeling the negative impact of all the new spending, the Benefits Division underperformed as a group, and for most of the benefits offices, the incentive program was a nonevent. However, my office and several others had performed and were owed significant dollars. In fact, had the bonuses been paid, they would have been more than what was paid to the divisions that had met their annual goals. When John realized what happened, he said, "No way."

Shortly after, I was working in my office when my assistant appeared at my door and asked if I would meet in the conference room with the staff and Mr. Cay. "Holy cow," I said. She called a meeting with the chairman of the company! I walked into a very awkward situation. With John sitting at the head of the conference table and every seat taken, I pulled a chair to the corner of the room behind John and sat down to watch the show. My assistant, never known for being tight lipped, proceeded to ask the chairman why the group had been misled all year and was not receiving the promised bonus.

John was believably shocked. "Where did this whole bonus idea come from? We have never done this before." I could tell he was struggling with the whole mess, and I chimed in that there was a written program that had been distributed to every employee in the Benefits Division. At first he could not grasp what was going on, so I got up, went back to my office, and retrieved a copy of the program. He was stunned! I genuinely believe that in his mind there was a potential bonus arrangement that may be implemented if business was good, but he had no idea that there was a formal program communicated to everyone. This goes to prove that talking is not necessarily communicating, nor is listening indicative of agreement. What a big company mistake, not at all the Palmer & Cay way. Once again, we missed Lew Oden; he would never have let this happen.

What happened after the meeting was also very telling about how Palmer & Cay had changed. In light of the bonus fiasco, the producers in the group unanimously decided we would share our regular production bonuses with the nonproducers in the office. That would require redirecting some money through accounting. When this idea was presented to Ray Slabaugh and Dave Morgan, the answer came back a firm NO! They were worried about what repercussions that decision may have with the rest of the offices that had not earned a bonus. Seems like people were worrying about the wrong things.

Chapter 20

You Can't Make More Than Me

Along with the bonus problem, I would soon encounter a separate issue concerning my own compensation. As in most companies, each year managers prepare budgets for the upcoming year that are reviewed and tweaked by senior management. In many large companies, management usually artificially raises the revenue number in the budget and slashes expenses to the point that the budget does not resemble reality but meets the narrative that management wants to present. This kind of budgeting is also what causes people to take actions that wind up in the press with everyone asking why people would do such a terrible thing.

With the fiscal year coming to a close, I traveled to Richmond to review my proposed budget for the next year. Ray Slabaugh, Dave Morgan, and the controller for the Benefits Division were in the meeting. I had put in my budget a small raise for myself and was ready for what I was sure would be coming as pushback. To my surprise, not only did I get resistance, they wanted me to take a reduction in salary with some weak promise of more bonuses if things went well. Having just been through two bonus issues (one for my people and the one when my bonus was reduced), I was not about to go along with this proposal.

I asked, "Why should I take a cut in pay?"

Ray responded, "Well, Ron, you are the highest paid person in the division."

"So, if not me, then who? Someone has to be the highest paid."

"But you are higher paid than me and Dave."

"Ray, my compensation is based on results built up over fourteen years."

"We just think you should do this, and we have talked about it with Mike Crowley."

"Let me get this straight," I said, "you want me to go back and tell my wife that after having my best year in the insurance business, leading the largest and most profitable benefits office in the whole company, and making the introduction that led Doug Hutcherson to close the largest sale in the history of the Atlanta office, I am having a pay cut?" I was incredulous!

By now Ray's head was slightly bobbing up and down like it did when he embarrassed himself in our first meeting. His mouth was moving but no sound was coming out. He knew right then I would not agree to his plan for me, and I knew he had not taken this to John Cay or Jim Meathe, or he would have already played that card. I also suspected that it was not presented to Mike Crowley as a "pay cut" for Ron, but rather a "redesign in compensation." In my opinion this was all about Ray's ego; Dave and the controller did not have anything to say. This was a big-company type of maneuver that I had seen before. Ray could not stand the fact that someone reporting to him was higher paid. The reality in most companies is that top performers on formula compensation plans usually make more than the president or other senior managers.

The best I could figure was that Ray may have felt so emboldened by Jim Meathe taking over the company that he decided the timing was right to make a move and put me in my place. From one of my consultants, I already knew he wanted to break up my group in Atlanta and carve out some of my responsibilities. Interesting that this would come from a man who had been pushed out of a position in a national firm by the board of directors. This news came from a lawyer who was on that board and had no respect for Ray's management ability. Ray was not even the founding partner of Slabaugh, Morgan, and White. That Slabaugh founder was Ray's brother, Jim Slabaugh. Ray joined the company after Jim Slabaugh, Dave Morgan, and Julie White were already in business.

Anyway, for a number of reasons, I was not worried on the trip back to Atlanta. First, for most of the time since Palmer & Cay bought Slabaugh, Morgan, and White, Lew Oden had really been the head of the Benefits Division even though Ray and Dave held the title. Nothing happened without Lew's okay. Second, when Ray would mention in meetings of the previous board that I was positioning to take his job, both Karen Lehman, our CFO, and David Hofele, our chief legal counsel, would voice contrary opinions. And the last reason I was not concerned was that I knew how both John Cay and Jim Meathe felt about me and my staff; Ray would have lost that battle. Still, it was annoying to put up with this political posturing after so many years of mostly harmony in Palmer & Cay. I did not accept the plan that was presented to me, and the issue was never discussed again.

Chapter 21

A Ghost from the Past

Once again, an incoming call on my cell phone while driving down the street brought an interesting exchange that had the potential for disaster.

"Ron, it's Jim. How you doing?"

"Great, Jim, what's up?"

"Listen, someone gave me a tip on a benefits guy who wants to join us here in Atlanta, said he is good."

"Really, Jim, who is it?"

When he told me the name I immediately became alarmed because this person had worked for me before at another company, and I was not about to bring him on at Palmer & Cay. After I originally hired him, this individual went from a fairly good insurance broker to, over time, the most divisive person on my staff. He wanted to be in management so badly that he became a pain in the ass to everyone in the organization. Finally, my boss arranged quietly behind the scenes for a transfer of this management wannabe to a city far, far away. Ironically, that is exactly how he had come to Atlanta in the first place—being transferred by a previous employer from another city under the same circumstances. Obviously, this most recent transfer had not ended well. As someone said, "He was there two years and never peed a drop." I think that means he did not accomplish anything. Now I was faced with the choice of going against my own will or bucking the president of my company.

"Jim, I already know this guy. He worked for me for seven years, and I don't think he is a fit for us. Let me explain . . ."

Before I could say another word, Jim interrupted me. "Ron, say no more. If you don't want him, you don't have to take him. I was just passing on information given to me. It is totally up to you, your decision."

Wow, I felt like I had just dodged a bullet! Jim's reaction was not what I expected in this situation and reaffirmed my belief that he respected what I had accomplished at Palmer & Cay. By now Jim knew some of my people and had recognized our results. His reaction was very much appreciated, as things could have gotten really ugly. I would not have backed down.

Although I still wanted to have hope for the company's future, this one positive exchange was not enough to offset my feelings of gloom.

Chapter 22

End of First Year

My morning rounds had become very depressing. Almost everyone that I spent time with was unhappy, mad, or scared. Like me, Tom Coker was carefully watching the numbers and comparing them to what management was putting out. He had the same access as me, and his conclusion was that the plan would not work. Even if our people could bring on the new business called for in the plan, which would have been unheard of in our industry, there was no way we could handle that volume of business in the time allowed with the resources available. The expenses were piling up, the goals too big, and the time too short. It was just not probable and, more importantly, not possible.

In less than a year, Palmer & Cay had been transformed from an organization distinguished by an optimistic, feel-good story of success, strong employee loyalty, and pristine reputation to one of doubt and apprehension. However, we still had our public reputation, as the outside world had no idea what was going on behind the scenes. Many of our own employees who either did not have access to the data or who had bought into the new regime still viewed Palmer & Cay positively. Those of us who were managing a budget, however, knew a different story. Many client accounts, especially in the Property/Casualty Division, renew on January 1 of each year. By this point, the new people and new offices had close to ten months to bring in their accounts, and it just was not happening. The company was already in trouble. Because commercial insurance is mostly renewed in January with a smaller number in July, it was apparent we would miss, for the most part, an entire renewal season.

John Cay went ahead with the announcement of the new ownership structure that would be implemented in the new year. My mood was not improved by an in-depth article published in *Cigar Aficionado* about the Seagram's fortune. The current Seagram's heir in control of the empire brought in a new CEO from France who wanted to convert the company from a beverage company into an entertainment conglomerate. With a complacent board of directors, this new executive made a slew of bad acquisitions, loaded up the company with debt, and lost much of the value of the enterprise. Billions of dollars were lost. Despite the difference in size, the parallel of the Seagram's story to Palmer & Cay was not hard to see.

One of the first signs of financial trouble in an organization is when the financial reports start to change or become unavailable. We were starting to experience both. A summary by city or division is not the same as the detailed profit-center reports we were accustomed to getting. I knew they were still being produced and would get accounting in Savannah to send me a copy, which they did until they were told not to send it out. That did not stop me— I just asked John Cay when I saw him to let me have a look. He would give it to me to make a copy for my use. I guess management figured out from things I said that I knew more than I should, and they eventually asked John not to give it to me. He disregarded their instructions but told me to keep it quiet.

The news was really bad. The plan was not working. Most people with any sense knew it and most of the conversations revolved around our problems. Management, on the other hand, kept pumping out sunshine in the form of overly optimistic projections. Early in the year around the first anniversary of Jim Meathe's arrival, I was engaged in a conversation with Frank Eldridge (an account executive who worked with Fran Millar) when he pointed out that we were already in deep trouble with little hope of recovery under the present management. It had only taken around twelve months to achieve this status. He went on to point out that if Palmer & Cay had been a larger company, we would be all over the news. As I listened to Frank, I thought to myself, *This is what happens to people you read about, like Seagram's. It is not supposed to happen to us.*

Tom Coker had another bent on the story when I walked into his office one day feeling particularly blue. He looked up from his desk with a serious look on his face and asked if I heard that Jim Meathe was changing the company logo. I had had many laughs with Tom and knew his cadence well enough to anticipate this could be a setup.

"Yeah, he is getting rid of the old steamship. The new logo is going to be a submarine!" At that, he held up a hand-drawn picture of a submarine underwater. It was one of those things that is so silly you can't help but laugh your butt off. As in all humor, it was based on a certain amount of truth that wasn't one bit funny.

While all this was going on, I was still trying to make things work. It was around this time that I brought one of my close friends into the company. Lee Barnett was an investment guy who would fit in well with Vic Bell, the head of our investment group. Even though I was sure things were really bad, I was still holding out hope that John would take back the company or, when we were forced to sell, the new leaders would bring us back to reality. As part of the interview process, all professional-level employees now had to go through an interview with Jim Meathe. When I asked about this new step, I was told that the board wanted to slow down the volume of hiring and become more strategic and more selective with each hire.

When Lee returned from his interview I asked, "How did it go?"

"Strangest interview I have ever had—not really an interview," he said. "The man must have ADD, because he could not stay on the subject. He talked about his new cashmere socks and how fragile they were. Then he would call out for Sue and she would come rushing into the room. He wanted coffee or something to drink or for her to find his glasses, which were on his desk. We really did not talk business."

I responded, "Welcome to my world."

When Lee was hired, I began to have second thoughts about bringing in friends while having such misgivings about the future of the company. I never dreamed I would ever be in such an uncomfortable position.

Part II

The Second Year
(January–December 2004)

Chapter 23

Hiring Mel

As if things weren't strange enough at Palmer & Cay, one of the more bizarre occurrences took place the week of the Super Bowl in 2004. Through word of mouth, I learned that a former employee from a previous company was about to go to work at Marsh as a senior producer. Mel had worked for me briefly fifteen years earlier and we stayed in touch intermittently. So what the heck, I decided to see what he was up to, since I knew he had recently had an unfortunate experience with another major brokerage firm. It turned out that Marsh was putting together a team in Atlanta to go after the large national accounts. Our former associate John Carswell, who reentered the insurance business when his noncompete contract expired, was part of the team. John was no kid, probably in his seventies, so I guess Marsh wanted young Mel (in his late forties) to help provide balance. In fact, Mel had always been an "elephant hunter," even in his youth. Older businessmen always liked Mel and would take a fatherly interest in helping him. For example, one of his accounts was the pharmaceutical/personal-products conglomerate out of New Jersey, Johnson & Johnson. That one account had over one hundred thousand employees.

In our telephone discussion, I expressed concern about Mel signing up with another large broker. He had experienced that environment before and knew how stifling it could be. Plus, his most recent experience left a bad taste in his mouth and a lawsuit that was still in litigation.

When I got off the phone with Mel, I went upstairs to see Frank Beard. Frank was immediately all over it because we needed positive news. He quickly got me in front of Jim Meathe and, naturally, Jim was beside himself for a chance to hire a big-time producer right from under Marsh. It was just more than he could stand. When I pointed out that this was Friday and Mel was to report to Marsh on the following Monday, Jim had me call Mel and set up a meeting for the two of them on Sunday afternoon. Jim wanted to handle this on his own and I was not included. Just as well; I had to help Jeannie prepare for our Super Bowl party.

On Monday morning, I learned that Jim had talked Mel into joining Palmer & Cay instead of Marsh and that Mel would be breaking the news to the head of the Marsh office sometime that day. Around midmorning I was behind closed doors with one of my people when my assistant knocked and stuck her head in. "Ron, do you have a few minutes for Mel?"

That really took me by surprise; however, I figured he might be looking for advice as how to handle things at Marsh. I said, "Sure, put him through, but why didn't he call my direct line?"

She gave me a strange look and said, "He is not on the phone."

What in the heck was going on? "Well then, where is he?" She started laughing, to which I responded, "He is here? You mean here in the building?"

She kind of looked around and said, "He is here, right behind me!" In walked Mel.

After I cleared my office, I asked, "Mel, what in the heck is going on? When are you going over to Marsh to give them the bad news?"

"I was just there."

"And they let you leave? It was that easy?"

"Well, not exactly."

"What?" Now I was really confused.

"I left them a note."

"What do you mean, you left them a note?"

"There was nobody there to tell. None of the senior management was there, the head of the office was not there, John Carswell was not there, and HR didn't know what to do with me. My new office wasn't ready yet, so they put me in a conference room. I waited for an hour or so and was getting anxious. I found the girl copying the prospect list I had given them at the last meeting and got it back. Then I sat down and wrote a note explaining I had changed my mind and left it with the receptionist."

By now, I was laughing so hard that tears were rolling down my cheeks. I had known Mel to get himself into funny situations, but this was the best one yet. There were several other things I would learn later. One was that Marsh had already sent out a blast e-mail announcing the superproducer team and that Mel was joining the company. And, more important to me, was that I would be paying half of Mel's compensation out of my budget even though he would be a general producer operating outside of the Benefits Department. No wonder Jim didn't want me at the Sunday meeting; he was giving away my money. At least we were having a good time.

Chapter 24

Vice President of Everything

I never got to know Don Holmes. However, he was one of those people that everyone, when asked, would say was a "great guy." I wasn't able to determine if people's enthusiastic reaction to Don was because he really was a great guy, or if it was because they all knew he was a close friend of Jim Meathe's, or if they felt by saying he was a "great guy" they became part of the "in crowd" who must all agree on certain things. Anyway, good guy or not, I personally had no problem with Don since I didn't know him. It was his hiring to begin with and then his role in the company that caused my concern as a practical, bottom-line business person. The major problem was that in order to be close to his children, Don chose to live in Colorado with no intention of moving east. So, with 1,652 road miles separating Denver and Savannah, why not put Don in charge of the administrative functions for the company, all of which were based on the coast of Georgia? Even with today's advanced communication options, managing a group of people that far away makes no sense.

Originally, Don was hired in a business-development role for an outpost in the Rockies. Of course, this didn't make any practical sense either since almost the whole company was east of the Mississippi. We had no presence anywhere near Colorado to provide support for a Denver office, and finally, no one in the area had ever heard of or cared about Palmer & Cay. This had the appearance of providing a job for one of Jim's friends so that he could continue his business and personal relationship. This was clearly not a decision imperative to the operation of the company, but instead personal to Jim. We were wasting a professional-level position that could have been better used closer to home. Our pockets were not deep, which was a concept lost on Jim Meathe. A giant company like Marsh could afford as many people as they wanted, while Palmer & Cay needed to use resources wisely.

Don would go on to spearhead another expensive use of company money, which typified a total lack of understanding of the entrepreneurial environment we were in versus the big-company mentality he came from. Don would be put in charge of communicating the new company-compensation program. I suspected that Don had no background in commission-only sales. More on that to follow.

Chapter 25

Matrix Management

MEMO
FROM THE DESK OF ALAN C. GREENBERG

DATE: July 20, 1994
TO: Senior Managing Directors, Managing Directors, & Associate Directors
FROM: Alan C. Greenberg

Today's <u>New York Times</u> disclosed that a major company has declared "matrix management in our company is dead." The president of that company said "That statement is monumental." I must admit that the company involved with that style of management cannot be faulted for not giving it a fair trial because over the last four years this tool has helped them lose four billion two hundred million dollars.

The company is now going to try putting in place "a system that makes its top executives more clearly accountable for the success or failure of their divisions. No more interminable meetings before making a decisions. No more delays in replying to a customer's call for "help." This article made me realize how stupid I am because I did not know there was any other way to run a business but to make people accountable, make timely decisions and service the client.

Another year has come and gone. It was exciting and certainly one of our better efforts. We had major disappointments from certain associates, but maybe it will help us run a tighter shop. Our goal still remains— a high return on equity with integrity.

The above memo is from the book *Memos from the Chairman* by the legendary chairman of Bears Sterns Companies, Alan C. Greenberg. If after reading this memo, your guess is that Jim Meathe decided to implement matrix management at Palmer & Cay, then you would be right. I had had a taste of matrix management in a prior position, so it took me a while to figure out why Jim was intent on this approach. To begin with, let me explain as best as I can what matrix management is about. To start with, you need to think in terms of solid lines and dotted lines. That is because everyone in the organization has two persons to report up to on the organization chart. First, you have the person you report to as an immediate supervisor; that's a solid line. Then there is someone else that may also have responsibility for your professional performance, which is the dotted line. Somehow all this reporting is supposed to improve each person's performance, assuming there is any time left over for actual work. Needless to say, the organization charts for a company with matrix management are quite amusing with all the lines going in different directions. They look like something designed by the federal government. I am sure there are a number of different ways a company could set up the lines of reporting, but the gist of this approach is multiple reporting.

Very few companies actually undertake matrix management, and of those that are successful, I submit that they are successful *in spite of* matrix management for reasons other than this double-reporting scheme. Most likely, they already have superior talent, or an outstanding product, or a strong position in their marketplace. So why was Palmer & Cay moving in this direction? One day in a conversation with Jim Meathe, he unintentionally let the answer slip. By installing one of his people in a dotted-line position in each profit center, he could know what was going on all over the company and have a say in every decision. Not very streamlined, but effective if you are determined to micromanage. Besides an enormous waste of time, every decision requires two people to sign off. My experience from a morale standpoint was not very positive because it is hard to know who you should be pleasing, especially if there is a conflict between the two people your lines lead to. Instead of simplifying the lines of communications, we were adding another level of management. At Palmer & Cay we had always prided ourselves in a flat management structure. No one was more than a few levels from the top of the company.

Interestingly, no one at Palmer & Cay took this new management approach seriously; even the new people just shrugged it off. It made no sense and people really didn't understand it. I guess at some point in time it would have led to major issues; however, people just went about their work as if there were no change. What I still don't understand is why CEOs feel the need to implement new approaches that so obviously go against common sense when the current method is working very well. It is as if they wish to make changes simply for the sake of change. What about "If it ain't broke, don't fix it"? Maybe leaders with too much time on their hands have to create drama to make things interesting.

Chapter 26

The Disincentive Plan

As promised, management, apparently without any input from current executives or any evaluation of the existing plan, proceeded to design a new compensation plan. With the assistance of an outside consulting company—at no small cost—a sophisticated, big-company program was announced. It was probably one of the best disincentive programs money can buy. I had seen similar momentum-killing plans before, and this one ranked right up there with all the rest. It was basically the companion piece to matrix management, which emanated from the mind of some consultant as a science project with no empirical data to support its results. We already had a successful program that directly compensated people for quantifiable results, so why not change it to something that is harder to understand, more subjective, and less rewarding?

Again, think in terms of a matrix with boxes that are further subdivided. It's kind of like a piece of graph paper on which one axis (y) represents different levels of income and the other axis (x) represents levels within the y-axis. For instance, a person could be in the $100,000-per-year box and then, based on an evaluation, could be plus or minus a certain percentage. The plus-or-minus part would be determined by both objective factors, actual sales or service goals, and subjective factors such as leadership, community activities, industry participation, and so forth. The bottom line is that by jumping through hoops, working significantly harder, you may trade 50 percent more effort for 3 to 5 percent more compensation. What a deal! What if you are already working successfully to capacity? What if your direct supervisor has a different idea on the subjective requirements? What if you just want to do a good job without all the superfluous requirements? Not everyone wants to be an industry leader or mentor or community volunteer. My theory is that the real reason for matrix management and the accompanying compensation system is to demonstrate control by limiting compensation and opportunity while giving the false appearance of fairness.

Like matrix management, the new compensation plan was mostly ignored by the managers, an approach that would cause a considerable confrontation for Don Holmes at an upcoming meeting. The former big-company people just did not understand why entrepreneurs didn't follow in lockstep to management's edicts. Back at Marsh—or Aon or Willis—everyone just accepted whatever came down from Chicago or New York, which is why people left those firms to join Palmer & Cay in the first place. When Don presented this new plan to a group of managers, he received considerable pushback. In response, he kept repeating that the decision had already been made, so why were we acting like it was still up for discussion? He was there to talk about implementation, so everyone needed to comply. No one in the room accepted that decision, and I don't remember the compensation plan being implemented. Of course, that may have been because time was running out.

The real question that the board should have been asking was how much money and time was Palmer & Cay going to waste trying to turn the company into something that no one wanted. Every day all over the business world, talented people leave the big, bloated, bureaucratic companies in search of clarity, personal freedom, and economic opportunities. Freedom and opportunity were exactly what we had at Palmer & Cay, which in turn resulted in sustained success over many years. The new people were so arrogant about how much more they knew than we small-company yokels that they could not comprehend there was a better way of conducting business. Many of these people would go through their whole careers without experiencing the fulfillment of working in an environment where every day is a joy. The real reason senior management liked the big-company compensation plan was that they could tightly control the expense line on the budget by subjectively capping earnings, while they always got theirs from stock awards. We went from a simple system that everyone could understand to one that no one wanted or thought was good. And those folks were correct—the new plan certainly was not good!

Chapter 27

Tocqueville Society

Each year, most financial-service companies and much of the business world conduct charitable fundraising drives. Usually the United Way is the vehicle of choice with a goal of having everyone participate at some level. At Palmer & Cay, we would distribute the materials to all employees and leave the contribution decision up to the individuals. This year, there was a little surprise request for the executives aimed primarily at senior management. Jim Meathe was asking senior VPs to join the United Way Tocqueville Society. This was the first I had heard of such a thing. The Society has nine levels of giving, starting at $10,000 and going up to $1 million plus. Needless to say, this was a departure from past practices. Although the request was presented as a guideline, it is hard not to interpret an e-mail from the boss as anything other than an order.

There were a number of reasons why this was not Palmer & Cay's style. It felt more like something one would expect when working for a big corporate giant in New York, Boston, Philadelphia, or Chicago. First, this kind of management intrusion into the personal finances of employees did not fit with the Southern culture of minding one's own business. Second, most Southerners focus their charitable giving on their churches and their children's private schools. Anyone with children in private school knows that the tuition is just the beginning of the giving. Giving money to some large general fund to be distributed by people unknown lacks the personal touch. Don't get me wrong, we already participated in the United Way, just not at the level requested.

There was one more very important reason why joining the Tocqueville Society was not popular with longtime Palmer & Cay executives. Most of us were well compensated; however, our family budgets were pretty well set for our income level. We did not have room to peel off another $10,000 to give to charity. Many of the new, former-Marsh people had just received huge raises to join the company, and most were moving into lower-cost-of-living areas. They could afford the entry fee of $10,000. Since I was already supporting one private school, in the end I doubled my annual United Way giving, which was nowhere close to the guideline. Although we never heard another word about it, the whole incident contributed to the changing mood of the company.

Chapter 28

Failure to Capitalize

The plan all along was to fund the growth of Palmer & Cay with financing from the major insurance companies with which we placed our clients' insurance. Our reputation in the marketplace was excellent, and the insurers were standing in line to help us. One of the reasons they wanted to help Palmer & Cay and other similar firms was that the distribution channels for their commercial products were becoming too concentrated in the handful of national insurance-brokerage firms. Insurance-company money comes at more attractive rates and terms than money from the big banks. Everything started out well until we were turned down by virtually every lending insurance company we counted on. What happened to all the support promised by our good friends at the insurance companies? After all, we really needed the money to pay for the expansion that was already in place.

Well, it appeared that Marsh really didn't like us stealing all their employees and then suing them. Palmer & Cay placed millions of dollars of insurance premiums with the insurance companies, while Marsh placed billions of premium dollars with the same companies. For most of the insurance companies, Marsh was their biggest source of business. It did not take long, either officially or unofficially, for the insurers to get the message that lending Palmer & Cay money could be bad for their business.

Before the expansion, Palmer & Cay had a debt of around $12 million, which represented approximately 9 percent of annual revenue. This very manageable amount was used to fund acquisitions of smaller brokerages and short-term capital needs. In past years, we had been able to pay off debt way ahead of schedule with no problem, giving us a great relationship with the lenders. Under the new, aggressive expansion, however, the debt would reach as high as $60 million, or 43 percent of annual revenue. At 43 percent of revenue, we were at a point that was economically unsustainable and probably the reason we were in violation of our existing loan covenants. The debt ratio was catastrophically high for not just Palmer & Cay, but unsustainable for any financial-service company. While this debt was being incurred, revenue growth stalled and we were spending $250,000 a month on legal fees fighting Marsh. Where was the board? Or for that matter, where was our "big-time" Wall Street CFO when we needed favorable loan agreements? We were now at the mercy of the less-preferred big banks, primarily Wachovia out of North Carolina.

A word about Wachovia: the Wachovia we found ourselves dealing with was formed when First Union Bank bought Wachovia. The latter's reputation was so much better than First Union that the decision was made to keep the Wachovia name after the acquisition and ditch the First Union moniker. However, the bank was still controlled by the same people with the reputation for being difficult. These were our new business partners!

Chapter 29

The Partnership Meeting

One of the agonizing decisions each professional-level associate faced that spring and summer was how much to invest in the new partnership. There was a minimum requirement for whatever level a person found him or herself in. For example, as a senior VP/managing partner, my minimum was around $350,000. Given my longevity and position, that would not be a problem for me, as my ownership in company stock was already well beyond that point. However, many new partners would need to find the money somewhere or borrow it from a bank. Many productive work hours were lost while people discussed their options. A number of us were worried about the future of the company, and leaving money on the table to justify a position in the organization was a difficult decision. Most of us went back and forth trying to decide.

One day I found Mike Crowley visiting in Atlanta and cornered him to get his point of view. His response, while not trying to sound negative, was that it would be okay to take some money off the table at this time. As big a team player as he was, this statement was telling.

In looking back at my history with Palmer & Cay, I recalled a time when John Cay did not want employees heavily investing in the company. He worried about having the responsibility for other people's financial security. He encouraged everyone to diversify their investments. When I first started buying company stock, there were controls on how much one could purchase. Every sale was approved by senior management, and not everyone was allowed to become a shareholder. A person had to contribute to the success of the company before becoming eligible. Now it seemed that everyone would be allowed in, and right at a time when the risk appeared to be increasing.

Tom Coker, never a believer in the new regime, decided to sell almost all his stock back to the company. Tom Bennett, I believe, kept only the minimum required to be a partner. I took a third out and figured that even if the company failed I could recoup the rest when we were forced to sell to a competitor. Most people kept at least enough stock for the minimum required to be a partner.

With the new structure in place, a partnership meeting was called in September. To begin with, there were 128 partners, only 8 of whom were based west of the Mississippi. So where to have the first partners meeting? You guessed it: Dallas, Texas. With support people, we were bringing close to 150 people who, except for the 4 in the Dallas office, would have to fly to Texas and come in the night before in order to attend a morning kickoff meeting the next day. Had the meeting been held in Atlanta, Charlotte, Jacksonville, or Savannah, at least half of the people would have driven, and many would have been spared an extra night in a hotel. When asked, the rationale for having the meeting in Dallas was to keep people's attention in a location where they would not be distracted by their daily responsibilities of sales and client service. We did not have the financial luxury of this mentality. For a company already facing grim financial results, the partnership meeting in Dallas made no sense; once again, a big-company move without regard to costs.

The timing of the partner meeting coincided with a client visit I had scheduled in Plano, a suburb of Dallas, so I went out two days early. After having dinner with my client the night before the partnership meeting, I arrived at the hotel around 9:30 p.m. As expected, the bar was full of Palmer & Cay people who had arrived earlier for the meeting the next day. Also as expected, the room was segregated according to loyalties. There were groups of old Palmer & Cay people huddled up, and there were groups of ex-Marsh people gathered separately. Exhaustion was setting in after flying to Dallas and spending all day with my client, deterring me from staying in the bar for long. However, before going to my room I spent a half hour with some of the guys from Savannah. The mood was awful; they were very unhappy with what was going on in the company over the last year. I could sense that this whole partnership event was a bad idea.

In the light of day the next morning, things did not look any better. The look on everyone's faces and the tone of the conversations were disquieting. A presentation by Bobby Reagan did nothing to improve the mood. Reagan and Associates was the firm that provided the annual valuation to set the share price for the company stock. With the fiscal year ending on June 30, they had almost three months to prepare for this meeting, and yet the valuation was not complete. They offered some excuses for the delay, which was met with suspicion. The revenue numbers for the year were $148 million with $8.5 million in after-tax profit. A 6.5 percent profit in the insurance brokerage business is not a good thing. We were feeling the results of the last year under the new regime.

The revenue projection for the next year was $189 million with a 21.87 percent pretax profit. Anyone with budget-management experience in our business knew that the projections were not realistic. Actually, they were pie in the sky with no hope of achievement. This was typical big-company budgeting: Overstate the goals and then spend twelve months thinking up the excuses for failure. Another disturbing fact to come out of the meeting was the announcement that we were already in violation of several of our loan covenants. While this fact was shrugged off as a technicality and no big deal, it certainly was not reassuring.

When Jim addressed the gathering, he grumbled that Rob Ellis, the company wordsmith and in-house comedian, had labeled the just-ending business year a "losing season." The most interesting part of the meeting was a joint question-and-answer session with both John Cay and Jim Meathe on the stage at the same time. To my surprise, it was one of the new guys who caused the biggest stir when he addressed the two leaders, telling them they needed to get on the same page, to which many others chimed in as to what should be done. At the end of the day when everyone shuffled out of the room, no one was happy.

Cocktails preceded dinner that evening. After the meal came my favorite part of the event. Each year at the sales retreat, Rob Ellis led the company in the Palmer & Cay oath. Everyone—including Jim and John—stood up and raised their right hand and repeated the oath written by Rob. It always started with Rob saying, "I state your name," to which everyone responded "I state your name" instead of filling in their name at the appropriate place. Even after a number of years, I still found this hysterical. I guess it was the juxtaposition of this high-achieving group of men and women, many of whom had advanced degrees, acting out in unison what amounted to an *Animal House* skit. For the body of the oath, Rob always threw in whatever was topical in business or culture at the time. For this oath, the last line was "So help me

Wachovia!" in reference to the bank currently lending funds to the company. I am not sure from the looks on their faces that either one of our leaders found that sentiment to be all that funny.

Speaking of oaths, one of the interesting things to come out of the partnership meeting was a partner directory. It had all the partners listed along with pictures, contact information, and their specialties. Up front on page seven was something called "The Palmer & Cay Way." It listed the typical corporate platitudes about our values. In light of our current corporate approach, I wondered if anyone had read that page.

The next day Tom Bennett left early, but I talked with him on the sidewalk before he left and found him miserable. He had the look of someone who hit the end of the line. There was a change in Tom's demeanor that I keenly felt. For one thing, our frequent talks out on the smoking balcony went from almost every day when we were both in town to me not being able to find him. Often, we would both be the last ones in the office at the end of the day, which was another opportunity to visit. Now it was rare to see him anywhere near the office. Tom's former manager was with one of our competitors, and many people wondered why Tom was still around. I feared the worst, as his behavior had clearly changed.

Later, when we saw the final numbers for the last fiscal year, those of us who were shareholders lost around 11 percent in the value of our stock. For me, that represented a retirement condo at the beach or perhaps a small farm in the mountains of North Georgia. This was when reality set in and my anxiety level increased dramatically.

Chapter 30

New Atlanta Manager

The Atlanta office had been without a manager for over a year. The previous manager left in the last reorganization when he did not get the position that Frank Beard was recruited for from the outside. Frank was, in essence, working two jobs while the company looked for a new Atlanta manager. Typically, the manager of a large insurance-brokerage firm needs to be someone well known in the industry and, hopefully, with a good local reputation, someone who knows the territory and is familiar with the history of the major accounts in the market. The ideal candidate would be a member of a prestigious club and a large church, and active in charity work. The target for Palmer & Cay was the local manager of one of the largest insurance companies with which we placed business. He looked the part, was the right age, and met most of the requirements. The only problem was that he was not interested in the job. I am sure his ego enjoyed the attention during the many meetings, dinners, and conversations; however, when he sat down and thought it through, we could not offer him the kind of guarantees that would offset what he had built up in his current position.

There were a number of people already on site who were interested in the Atlanta manager's job, including me. When I spoke to Frank Beard about it, he advised me that it was not in the plan, as they were speaking to someone in Chicago to move to Atlanta. Someone from Marsh! Some weeks later, I was asked to be a good soldier and attend an intimate dinner at a high-end expense-account restaurant in Buckhead. The purpose of the dinner was to entice the guy from Chicago to join Palmer & Cay in Atlanta.

Four couples were at the table, including the guest of honor, Mike Liss, and his wife. My wife and I were seated between Fran Beard and his wife and Bill Lenhart and his wife. We were sitting directly opposite the Lisses. The dynamics were more than interesting, as we already knew that Mike's wife was against any move from Chicago, especially to the South. She, not being a Southerner, did nothing to hide her true feelings as everyone went through their paces to be nice and uplifting.

"The weather is better in Atlanta, traffic really isn't too bad, home values are good compared to Chicago, schools are great, closer to vacation spots, blah, blah, blah . . ." All night long. She barely responded. Mike, on the other hand, was trying to control himself while eating it up. He was being given his own operation and the largest office in the company, the flagship, if you will.

Partway through the night, Will Underwood (an Atlanta producer) showed up at the table by himself. Will had latched onto Bill Lenhart right from the start, and the two of them and their families became close friends. Bill must have alerted Will of the dinner, as he was not on the invite list for the evening. It was interesting for me to watch the politics at play as Will's loyalty moved from Palmer & Cay to the new management. He was accepting the change without understanding what was happening to the company. As a salesman, he was not privy to the financial information that was available to managers. Like many people both inside and outside of the company, he had no idea as to the extent of our problems.

By the date of the dinner, I had seen enough of the new regime to have a foreboding sense of things to come, and sitting there that night I felt a certain amount of sympathy for Mike, not to mention small pangs of guilt for my part in what we were doing to him and his family. This also would not end well, but at the time of the dinner it was not too late for them to cut and run. On the way home, I explained to Jeannie what was going on with the company and predicted that Mike would take the job over his wife's objections.

Mike had been handpicked by Jim Meathe with no one else even considered. Jim predicted to me that I would like him, and to my surprise, he was right. Mike was a stocky, baldheaded man who resembled the actor Michael Chiklis, who starred in the TV shows *The Commish* and *The Shield*. Actually, he carried himself like a commissioner. He was a very intelligent, quick-witted people person with good common sense. We worked well together. Mike's best trait may have been his sense of humor. One of the funniest Mike stories was one he told about a meeting in New York when he was with Marsh. It was a gathering of managers from around the country. In one session, a national executive addressed the group by declaring, "This is going to be the year of the customer," to which Mike asked, "What do we tell them last year was?"

Mike was not the problem for the Atlanta office. Most people came to view him as I did. The real problem was with Jim Meathe and all the other outsiders whose arrogant attitudes were hard to take. They produced no business, had no time for anyone outside their own group, and showed no respect for what had been accomplished at Palmer & Cay. They could be seen whispering to each other, and when they thought no one was looking they slipped in their little, secret handshakes. Was this for real?

Mike and I did disagree on one thing that I could never get him to understand. He wondered why everyone of the old guard was so resentful. I explained that we had all paid our dues to be here and the new guys hadn't, to which he replied, "Everyone paid their dues somewhere." My answer to that comment was that many of us passed up other opportunities to stay and build something special. This new group was following Jim for more money, or they were running away from Marsh. There is a big difference in a commitment to a long-term effort to build a company versus running to a company for more money. That was one of the factors that I always considered in hiring a professional-level associate: Is this person embracing an opportunity, or are they just running from a bad situation?

When Mike showed up in Atlanta, I made a point of spending part of each day with him. While he had responsibility for the overall office, I managed approximately 40 percent of the revenue and reported through the Benefits Division in Richmond. It was imperative that we worked well together, as we faced common issues in our day-to-day activities. Also, Mike was fun to be around and someone I could relate to from a management perspective. On his second day in Atlanta, Jim asked him what he was going to do with the office, to which Mike replied, "How do I know? I just got here! I am still learning my way to the restroom."

Chapter 31

The Second Vegetable Truck

There is a well-known business story about two guys with a truck who were trying to make a go of bringing vegetables from the country to the city. The main problem with their business model was that they were losing one hundred dollars a truckload. They got together to discuss their problem and, after much discussion, decided that what they needed to improve the situation was a second truck.

With revenues stagnating and expenses rising, the only thing to do, apparently, was to rent an entire new floor in the building that housed the Atlanta office. Nothing like fifteen thousand square feet of class-A office space to make you feel good about yourself. So, we picked up a sublet vacated by some high-tech software company. The space was not contiguous to our existing floors. In fact, it was many floors away toward the bottom of the building. The configuration of the space was not suited to the needs of an insurance broker, except for the executive corner suite with the private secretarial space guarding the door. Of course, that became Jim's office.

The offices with windows were so small that they had to have built-in workstations to be functional. And there were many of them. I guess programmers don't need much space. We filled as many as we could with stand-alone departments such as Human Resources, Aviation, Personal Lines, and so on. Due to the design and lack of need, we could not make use of half the floor. The conference rooms, reception area, and break rooms remained dark for the most part. The space was gloomy, like walking through an abandoned building. The mood that the dark reception area created as you walked into the space added to the depression many of us were experiencing. This was not a bright, joyous, prosperous place.

The space example was totally contrary to how many well-managed businesses operate, including the previous Palmer & Cay model. We always tried to keep space down to around 250 square feet per employee. We would make do with what we had until it became unbearable, even in good times. All this extra expense was so that the president could have the executive suite he longed for. Again, where were the board, the CFO, real businessmen, the adults?

Chapter 32

RIMS

The big industry event for insurance brokers and consultants is hosted by the Risk Insurance Management Society (RIMS). The RIMS convention is a large, multiday meeting moved each year to a different city around the country. Insurance brokers and insurance companies go all out for RIMS with huge budgets based on their stature in the industry. The larger companies would have convention booths befitting their size, with hospitality headquarters in large ballrooms or special-event places such as aquariums, museums, mansions, or any place that might attract a crowd. There would always be food and drink, plus entertainment. A company the size of Palmer & Cay typically would rent out a local restaurant for the week as the hospitality center.

Why the big deal about RIMS? Corporations from all over the country send their risk managers to the meeting. Thousands of people attend. Not much business changes hands at the meetings; however, most brokers participate as a defensive matter. If you

are not there with your clients, then someone else will be
entertaining them and relationships get started. Since this is a
mature industry, everyone is calling on the same people and you
need to be protective of your client contacts.

Naturally, Jim Meathe expected Palmer & Cay to be over the
top for his first RIMS meeting as president. We had the corporate
booth reworked into a much larger space in the ship motif. We
were now competing with the big boys in size and floor location.
And to really get everyone's attention, we had Palmer & Cay
banners mounted on light poles from the airport in San Diego to
the convention center! Everyone would know that Palmer & Cay
was there. We were making a big splash, all while our financial
numbers were tanking. At least we were going out in style.

Benefits people usually do not attend RIMS meetings unless it
is in their hometown, so I was not there to see our little company
in all its glory. However, I did see pictures of the banners that
marked the way along the streets. They were nice looking and
about six feet tall. I figured since we already paid for them, why
not distribute a banner to each of our twenty-eight offices to
display as wall hangings in the reception areas? I mentioned this
idea to Jim and he really liked it, suggesting I see our national
sales manager about following through. I talked to Bill Lenhart
about this little project and followed up with e-mails and phone
calls. Like a number of other initiatives, nothing ever came of it. It
was bad enough to have spent all that money on RIMS while
business was not great, but then to not use items we had paid for
seemed wasteful to me. For the new management, money was no
object.

Chapter 33

Blowup with the President

When I received my budget for the next year after it went through the corporate management-approval process, my worst fears were realized. Compensation for producers was changing from a formula-based program to a more subjective, discretionary approach. This would be a fundamental change in the Palmer & Cay philosophy and would not be well received. Right away I knew there was only one place I could go with this problem, so I tracked down John Cay.

When we talked by phone he was entirely sympathetic to my concern and said he would address the situation. John was tight with money in many ways; however, when it came down to paying for performance, he never hesitated. I was confident he was on my side for this issue, but worried that he would once again cave to Jim Meathe and the board.

All evening I agonized over how I would deal with my producers if I was forced to go along with the new program. The next morning on the way to the office, I felt the need to do something I almost never did that early: I checked my voicemail. Maybe I anticipated what was waiting for me. There was a message from Jim Meathe.

"Ron, what are you doing talking with John?" it started. There were no pleasantries. "You need to understand, I am the president now. Come to my office first thing in the morning when you get in."

Well, it looked like I stepped in it, but good. Sitting at my desk a few minutes later, I made the decision to ignore Jim's message and go about my day. Less than five minutes later, my phone rang. It was Sue, Jim's secretary.

"Ron, would you have a few minutes this morning to meet with Jim before he leaves on a trip?" she asked nicely and my problem was not of her doing, so I responded that I would be right down.

I was so exercised about the injustice of the compensation decisions that I did not have the anxiety that one would normally have as I traveled down the elevator that morning for a confrontation with the boss. Actually, I was ready to go on the offensive. I walked in and Sue guided me to Jim's inner office. He stood up and before Sue could get back to her desk, he let loose with his barrage. Sue immediately wheeled around and rushed back to pull the door shut. The whole scene probably looked comical, but no one was laughing. I sat back and waited until he was done venting. When it was my turn, keeping my voice down, I calmly explained that if he wanted to change the system going forward, that was his prerogative; however, changing the formula for the year just ended was the company going back on its word.

Jim responded, "I have seen what your people make, and they are well paid."

"That's right, they are well paid, but that's not—"

Jim interrupted, "Well, see? We can agree on some things," and before I could respond he stood up and stuck out his hand for a shake. "Now let's move on and put this behind us." With that, he walked me to the door, and I was back out in the hall with nothing settled. The whole exchange lasted less than five minutes. I went back upstairs thinking to myself that at least I didn't get fired. Later in the afternoon when I was positive Jim had left town, I went back down to his office. I stuck my head in the door to see Sue sitting at her desk, typing. When she looked up, I said, "Sure did enjoy spending time with you and Jim this morning."

She broke up and we had a good laugh. "Usually I can get the door shut before he goes off, but he was fast today." We laughed again.

Chapter 34

Executive Coaching

Over the years I had been fortunate to have made a number of good hires. I would like to think my success was due to the time, effort, and study devoted to the task, although I am not ruling out my own sheer talent and good fortune. One of the all-time best decisions I ever made was bringing Kathy Van Zant into the company to head up a human resources–consulting practice. I met Kathy ten years prior when she was an HR executive for a large software company that became a client. As often happens in software, her company was bought out and they wanted Kathy to move from Atlanta to Charlotte. She had recently married and was not interested in moving, so she left that position to start her own consulting company. When I decided to start an HR consulting group, Kathy was the first person who came to mind. I got her to agree to at least meet for a discussion, which led to further conversations. I arranged for Kathy to meet with John Cay, which I was sure would go well. John was at his best when it came to laying out a vision of the company and drawing people in, a charming Southern gentleman all around. Like many people who have been on their own for a number of years, joining an organization could only be attractive if there are a certain amount of personal freedoms and a real opportunity for success. At Palmer & Cay, we offered both.

Kathy started work during the first week of April in the year before the new management. On one of the first days that week, she asked to see me behind a closed door. I was immediately alarmed, thinking that she had a change of heart about joining the company. She started out saying, "This is not an April Fools' joke."

From then on I don't remember breathing. Kathy had just been diagnosed with breast cancer! Since it was her first week on the job, she offered to resign immediately. My reflex response was "Absolutely not." I wanted her to stay, and if she was willing to work through it, so was I. The whole discussion about her staying or leaving took about two sentences, and we never talked about her leaving again. Kathy went on to have treatment, which included chemo and surgery and of course the loss of her hair. Through it all, she continued to work, never missing a beat. In fact, she was going to be the Palmer & Cay lead in our joint venture. Everyone was glad she stayed with the company, a truly impressive person.

About the time Kathy was recovering from cancer, her next big challenge was on the horizon. One day she again came into my office and closed the door. This time she immediately volunteered that she was not there to resign. Instead, she was there to give me a heads-up that the board had come directly to her with a confidential assignment. It would involve consulting time that would not include any compensation. What the heck?

Kathy had been asked to provide executive coaching for our president, Jim Meathe. Evidently, after a year and a half of his behavior, the board finally consented to take action. This came too late to save our relationship with one of Atlanta's finest law firms, too late for our former CFO, too late for the producers who had already left and, finally, too late for those who had yet to resign but were making plans. When Kathy finished telling me about her assignment, the question I wanted to ask the board was what kind of professional services company has to have the president coached on personal deportment? Are you kidding me? How embarrassing!

Although she was not excited about the situation, Kathy accepted the assignment for the good of the company. Two thoughts crossed my mind about this news. First, another needless waste of company money to have a senior consultant working for free. It is hard to make a profit from free work. Second, maybe Ian Robb (head of HR) could enjoy his weekends now in peace. Ian once told me he could not escape Jim, especially on Friday nights when he would get calls about anything that happened to pop into Jim's head. Rather than making notes for discussion later, Jim would just pick up the phone and call Ian no matter where he was, often multiple times. Once he received several phone calls while sitting in the stands, trying to watch a ballgame.

My experience with the president's behavior, for the most part, stayed cordial and somewhat professional. In an effort to shore up relationships with key executives, he started reaching out to certain individuals. I was invited to have lunch with him in an Italian restaurant on Peachtree Street. We had a pleasant time, mostly social with much of the conversation about lake houses. It turned out that we both had had houses on the same lake as Alabama football coach Nick Saban. Jim's house was on a lake in Michigan and mine was on a lake in the North Georgia mountains. Who knew we would bond on something so obscure? During lunch, his wife called on his cell phone, evidently wanting his immediate attention on something. I could only hear his end of the conversation, but whatever it was, he said in a very annoyed manner, "No, because it is called a job," and then ended the call. I guess that made her day.

This brings an interesting thought to mind. I read somewhere long ago that Southerners make up a disproportionate number of CEOs in the business world. The premise presented was that all other things being equal between two candidates, the one with the best social graces would be chosen. It seems to me that Palmer & Cay did the opposite. We went from Mike Crowley, the even-keel, smooth Southerner, to the bull in a china shop, Jim Meathe. Jim even bragged about how much glass he broke at Palmer & Cay. A lot of bravado with little results.

Chapter 35

Strange Happenings

There were strange things going on other than having to coach the president of the company on things that, as the book *All I Really Need to Know I Learned in Kindergarten* says, he should have "learned in kindergarten." I'm not sure where this one fits in the continuum of this narrative; however, it certainly is worth telling as a lesson in human behavior. It started in a phone conversation with one of my good friends who worked at Marsh. He and I had worked together for around ten years in a previous life and knew each other well.

"Hey Ron, I hear that Johnny Cay is gay," he said, followed by laughter.

"What are you talking about?" I asked. "Where did that come from?"

By now he was doing the laugh that I was very familiar with, the one where he says something that he really doesn't believe but is enjoying the irony of the misinformation. "Heard it from John

D. Carswell himself," my friend said, pronouncing the name formally as if officiating at some important event, all the while laughing up a storm.

"Well, I can tell you this: I know John Cay fairly well, and I am sure he is not gay. Please pass that on to Carswell."

John Carswell was a whole story unto himself. He was the former owner of the John D. Carswell Company in Savannah that Palmer & Cay purchased several years before I joined the company. In recent years, with his noncompetition agreement (as part of the sale of his company to Palmer & Cay) expired, he had partially reentered the insurance business, joining forces with Marsh. I was not sure what was behind this rumor talk. He probably figured he could call on former customers for their business, and a little rumor about John Cay's sex life couldn't hurt his chances. Since many of Carswell's ex-clients were in smaller, more conservative communities like Augusta, maybe he thought the rumors would give him an edge for their business. He also knew that John and his wife of many years were not the picture of lovebirds to the casual observer. Mimi was seldom seen at company events outside of Savannah society. That, along with John's affinity for English haberdashery, especially bow ties, made him an easy mark for Carswell to leave false impressions. In the big picture, I don't think any of this really mattered, it is just curious what people will do in the business world.

Interestingly, John Carswell was a person with a past who, after achieving financial security and surviving his own scandalous marital situation, turned to religion, like many successful men. When I first joined the company, I began receiving in the mail at home those small, grainy leaflets sent out by Evangelical Christian groups. Checking around the company, I was informed that John Carswell (this was when we were still Palmer & Cay/Carswell) added each new employee to the mailing list of his church. So, how does starting sexual rumors about others square with his faith? Probably not very well.

Upstairs, I learned I was not the first person to pick up this rumor. Both Tom Coker and Phil Maddox were aware of what was going around. Hard to stay ahead of those two. Phil was especially upset by the whole situation. Where I was reluctant to bring this to John Cay's attention, Phil had already talked with John, encouraging him to confront Carswell. John Cay was very good at not being distracted by the noise and told Phil to ignore it all. I was told that eventually John Cay had his lawyer call Carswell and after the conversation, the innuendos stopped and the whole thing died out. Just another day in the business world.

So, what was this rumor really about? I feel there may have been three issues at play here, of which taking business from Palmer & Cay was the least important. The other two had to do with professional jealousy and bitterness over a failed business scheme. It must have been hard for John Carswell to look back at what John Cay had accomplished in the years since The Carswell Company was purchased by Palmer & Cay. After all, The Carswell Company had been the larger of the two at the time of the merger, and within a short period the Carswell name was dropped as Palmer & Cay exploded with success. The other issue was much more subtle. First, it is important to understand that many businessmen in Atlanta at that time were feeling like they missed a tremendous Internet opportunity by not investing in WebMD. The young founder of WebMD, Jeffery Arnold, a Georgia native, became a billionaire while still in his twenties. Everyone in the business community was looking for ways to replicate Arnold's success with the Internet. As a successful entrepreneur, John Cay was approached by many people as a potential financier of new business ideas. Thus, it was not surprising when John Carswell approached John Cay with an Internet-investment opportunity.

Frank Beard was assigned to investigate the plan and, since it involved health insurance, I was asked to participate in the initial meeting to be held in our main conference room. The basic idea to be presented was an Internet site for the purchase of individual health insurance. John Carswell himself led the delegation of a half-dozen people. The meeting started with introductions rotating clockwise around the table. Since I was sitting to the right of Frank Beard, I would be last to speak. Aside from Carswell, there were bright, young guys with backgrounds in technology, accounting, advertising, and public relations. Not one representative from the insurance industry! They were, however, throwing out names like Blue Cross Blue Shield, Aetna, Cigna, and other health-insurance organizations. When it became my turn, I introduced myself as an insurance broker of employee-benefits plans. My only question for the group was what insurance companies had agreed to participate with this plan, and what they were saying about how they would underwrite the applications. Crickets . . . all you could hear were crickets. They had no commitments from any insurers. In other words, they had no product. They were a marketing machine with nothing to sell. I did point out that in health care, finding customers was not a problem. Finding a company to take the risk was the real issue. Tsk-tsk, didn't I know that the Internet was so vast that you would only need a little sliver of it to get rich?

After the meeting adjourned, I was assigned to go with John Cay's son Jack to tour the offices of this Internet company. Of course, they were in class-A office space at Pershing Point, right on Peachtree Street. During the tour, we came to an area filled with a dozen young people taking down information from computer monitors on the wall. When I asked, it was explained that they were completing insurance applications on paper from information submitted to the website. This was really low tech. Apparently, at the time it was either against the law to submit applications to the insurance companies electronically or they just would not accept them in that form. When we returned to our office, John Cay asked how it went, and I explained what we witnessed. John started in with "The Internet is so vast . . ." I interrupted him and said we should keep an eye on this situation, as I really liked their space and it would be available soon.

Palmer & Cay never invested in the harebrained scheme, but John Carswell may have lost money. Therefore, my belief is that he further resented John Cay. Starting a rumor may have been, in part, payback for not taking the leap with Carswell on the failed Internet scheme.

Government Investigations

As if things weren't bad enough, other issues unrelated to the company changes kept popping up. One such issue was something started in New York by State Attorney General Elliot Spitzer. Spitzer was an ambitious politician who was making a name for himself on the backs of the misery he was causing large companies operating in New York state. His actions amounted to legal blackmail through prolonged, baseless government investigations without regard to the merits or deleterious effect it would have on the average worker. The investigations took so much time and asked for so much information that they were a penalty in and of themselves. Almost everything Spitzer pursued would be thrown out by the courts, but not before costing many executives their careers, and due to the financial impact of his charges, costing the jobs of many innocent, uninvolved employees. Later on, Spitzer would distinguish himself as governor of New York by an affair with a prostitute in a Washington, DC, hotel. Employing a prostitute is the very charge he made against many men back in New York. To top things off, Spitzer paid for the hooker's services with a credit card. What an ego!

When Spitzer turned his attention to the insurance industry, one of the problems his staff identified had to do with commission arrangements that guided the placement of commercial insurance to certain insurance companies. These commission arrangements had not been reported to the policyholders (clients), and therefore it was determined they were not in the best interest of the customer. There were really only two insurance brokers, Marsh and Aon, large enough to pull off this arrangement with any real impact. Although the premium numbers were large, within these two organizations the people involved were relatively few. Nevertheless, by the time Spitzer was through, the whole industry was made to pay in a number of ways. Stock values plummeted, retirement plans were hurt, and some companies suffered layoffs. The disruption caused by Spitzer was several magnitudes above the allegations against these companies. Like a typical politician, Spitzer could not be concerned about the damage he caused, including layoffs, since he was aiming for the governor's job. It is important to note that after his personal scandal drove him from the governor's office, he was given a TV show on CNN. Not sure what that says about our society and the importance of notoriety over achievement.

So how did all this come into play at Palmer & Cay? The Insurance Department of Georgia, like many others across the country, began to investigate insurance brokers by way of interviews and commission audits. Since we were the largest independent (privately owned) broker in the state, we were high on the list. Our management was not concerned about having the same problems as Marsh or Aon, but you should always be wary anytime there is an investigation. I was especially concerned since my group-insurance practice had an unusually large amount of bonus commissions that, on the surface, could be confused with what the investigators wanted to find. On the positive side, I knew that the investigators would not be looking for a problem in the benefits side of our business.

When the state investigator showed up on our doorstep, he went right to the commercial division for the investigation. Benefits was last on his list, and I was the last manager in Atlanta to be interviewed. Needless to say, there was a slight pucker factor on my part going into the interview. To make things worse, the interview would take place on the dark, half-empty floor below that we had just acquired. Not exactly a comforting place.

The interview was very informal, and the interviewer was spring-loaded to finish and leave the premises. I am not sure I was in there for more than two minutes, and I don't remember any questions of substance. To me, it seemed like:

"You really didn't do anything wrong, did you?"

Of course my answer was "No, sir."

That was the last we ever heard of that issue.

Around that time there was another, more serious potential problem that was directed only at me. I got a call one day from Tom Coker. "Ron, the SEC is here for an investigation and you are named as a person of interest."

Now, we are not talking about the Southeastern Conference of college sports. This SEC was the Securities and Exchange Commission, an agency of the federal government.

My response: "Yeah right!"

Tom: "No seriously, I am sending them down to your office. I just wanted to make sure you were there."

I gulped. "What do they want?"

"To see your books," he responded. "Good luck." *Click.*

A few minutes later a group of young, college-educated accounting types walked into my office. They needed a conference room and all my commission records from the last two years. They were neither antagonistic nor friendly. "Just the facts, sir."

I rightly assumed that the reason I was the person of interest was because as manager, I was licensed in almost every state and signed most of the commission agreements for our department. There were literally hundreds of them, none of which I had read. After a day and a half of looking at commission statements and reviewing our files, the manager of the group came into my office for an exit interview. I was asked about only one deposit of $2,000 out of around $16 million for the two years in question. That deposit was for an annuity contract that had the appearance of an investment product. I remember asking about the investment issue when I was asked to sign it two years prior, since there are strict licensing requirements for investment products that I was not about to go through for $2,000. In the end, they agreed that everything was legitimate and thanked me for my cooperation.

Later that evening, I was in the Atlanta airport heading out of town for a business trip when I ran into the same young people heading back to Chicago. As I said hello and goodbye to them again, I went on my way thinking, *That is your tax dollars at work.* The federal government sent four well-paid, college-educated people from Chicago to Atlanta, incurring flight, hotel, and meal expenses to make sure the $2,000 Palmer & Cay received was done so with the proper licensure. Had they called me from Chicago or identified what they were looking for when they arrived, I could have saved everyone time, money, and effort. I did come away from the encounter with a feeling of how wasteful government — any government — can be, and that people in legislatures don't understand the burden their good intentions place on private industry.

Why were all these strange things happening at once? Wasn't it enough that we were trying to save the company? I couldn't help but worry, *What's next?*

Chapter 36

The Wedding

John Cay's youngest son, Christopher, and I had become friends over several years. At one time, John had asked me to help talk Christopher into joining the company. Christopher is an independent individual and was reluctant to get into the family business. Besides, his older brother, Jack, was already heading up our New York office, which was a small start-up outpost. I would like to think that our discussions helped in some way to draw Christopher in at a time when he was looking at other options. As it turns out, he became successful at Palmer & Cay in our very selective Personal Lines Department. As a result of our relationship, I was invited to his wedding reception in September. The wedding was to be a big social event with the reception at one of Atlanta's finest country clubs, right in the middle of the Buckhead/Brookhaven area.

Around that time, the company was pretty much in turmoil. Financials were not improving, and everything seemed to be going wrong. As it happened, one of the bridesmaids was a young lady who worked for me. During the lead-up to the wedding and again afterward, we spoke often. From what she observed, the company's woes were never far from the topic of discussion between John, Jack, and Christopher. Evidently, they were engaged in numerous conversations about what to do with the company.

At the wedding reception, I was on the lookout for the two Atlanta board members who I was sure would attend as friends of the groom's father. Joe Rogers and Don Chapman walked in together. I tried my best to position myself without appearing to be a stalker. I even curtailed my alcohol consumption so that I might have a rational conversation without causing a scene. My goal was to speak to them directly to see if they realized the seriousness of the company's financial issues and to figure out what their current thinking was as board members. I planned to reintroduce myself to them and just have a casual talk.

It never happened.

They knew too many people in the large crowd and were never alone. I didn't have a chance to speak with them together. Of course, I could have called them individually to set an appointment, but that would have drawn more attention than an offhand, impromptu discussion at the wedding reception.

It was hard for me to understand how these two strong business leaders could sit by and watch this wonderful, old, successful company go down the tubes. How could they not understand what was so clear to many of us on the inside? The board had more information at its collective fingertips than what was available to the executives, especially with the restricted financial reporting of late.

Chapter 37

More Jumping Ship

Mike Crowley

Over the last year and a half, everything at Palmer & Cay had gone the wrong direction. Employees were openly talking about the company's problems. Many of us were encouraging John Cay to put an end to the madness by making changes before it was too late to recover. When I told him to take back the company and get rid of the three main players (two board members and the president), his response was "What do we do with all the people who have been hired? What about all the leases we now are responsible for?"

Of course, those would be significant problems, but we could've worked through them with good leadership. I suspected that John would not act due to the $15 million that we would have to pay the people who put us in this position. What about bringing Mike Crowley back as president? It was doable, not too late. People would rally around Mike.

When the announcement came, it was no surprise but still had an impact. Mike Crowley resigned. *Now* it was too late.

It took me quite a while to meld what I think happened with what I was told took place. What I was able to piece together started with John deciding to make a change. Apparently, John and Mike talked things through and John offered him the presidency back. I think they may have even had a drink over it. When Mike went home and shared the news with his wife, she may have raised the issue of compensation, specifically the no-cut contract that John had given Jim Meathe: $5 million guaranteed, win or lose.

The next conversation between the two men did not go so well when John refused to give Mike the same deal. And that was it. Mike resigned, and so went any hope of keeping things together. John displayed a trait that is common in many managers and corporate leaders. For unknown reasons, some executives underappreciate the advice or value of people in their own organization, while at the same time paying excessive attention to people from the outside. Often, they prefer to listen to someone from out of town carrying a briefcase.

Bennett Resigns

Although things were pretty bad already, Tom Bennett's resignation was another bombshell. In addition to being one of our best producers, he had been the only nonmanagement person on the board. Tom was well liked by most people and was clearly one of the informal leaders of the company. His leaving was a blow to both old and new management. One of the major concerns from a management perspective was that, up to this point, the company problems were known internally. Tom was a high-profile person in the insurance community. Accordingly, his resignation to join a competitor was a signal to the outside world that Palmer & Cay had serious problems. Palmer & Cay was not known for its people leaving, especially to join the competition, and this was the second time in just twelve months. Word began leaking out that things were not right.

For Jim Meathe, this was a personal disappointment. He genuinely liked Tom, and since the defections of last year he had been trying hard to keep things together.

For John Cay, it was more business than personal. I ran into him in the reception area just after Tom's announcement, and he asked me if I could talk Tom into changing his mind. I said no. When John asked why, I started to say because Tom was leaving due to personal conviction, not for money or position. Before I could finish my statement, someone walked up to us and interrupted the conversation. John turned away and that was the end of discussion. Nothing personal. No need to follow up.

Tom Coker Retires

It was no surprise when Tom Coker retired. He never bought into the whole "new company" that was being created. Tom watched the numbers carefully and often said we were in trouble. Strangely, he wanted no retirement function, no party, no lunch, and no drinks after work. We all thought that was a bit odd, but just assumed he felt bitter about how things were going.

Well, it turned out that he had a surprise that no one saw coming. A few days after retiring, word came back that Tom was at work the very next week over at McGriff Seibel, one of our competitors. A very short retirement, to say the least! This was the firm that our former Atlanta manager and Tom Coker's good friend went to and the firm that Tom Bennett had just joined. The next time I saw Tom, he explained that he felt guilty leaving Palmer & Cay under false pretenses; however, by retiring instead of resigning, he protected the value of the Palmer & Cay stock that remained in his name.

From time to time I would run into Tom Coker at a local diner, usually on Wednesdays for the fried chicken. On the other hand,

I did not see Tom Bennett again until one evening in December, coming out of a drugstore several blocks north of the office. He did not look well, which I took as being a result of his inner turmoil about leaving Palmer & Cay. He reminded me that it was not just a job, but part of his whole life. After all, as he pointed out, even his children did not know anything other than The Ship. The next thing he said really got my attention.

"You better hope they find a buyer before the company goes bankrupt, because if they don't, shareholders stand in line with all the creditors. Good luck then getting anything back."

In fact, under bankruptcy laws, shareholders come after all the creditors. He and I had seen this scenario played out a number of times in the business community. He was right, and this reality ruined my holiday season. I knew too much about the financial condition of the company, and bankruptcy was a definite threat. At that point, there was no news about selling the company.

With people leaving and Tom Coker retiring, why didn't I make plans to move on to another opportunity? The answer is simple: In my mind, I was an owner and had as much right to be at Palmer & Cay as anyone else in the company other than John Cay himself. After working relentlessly for sixteen years, at age fifty-seven I had made my stand. I had a strong identity with the company and felt a responsibility to all the people I had recruited to join our effort. Like with Tom Bennett, Palmer & Cay became my life. There was not much separation between my business life and my personal life. Working at Palmer & Cay was not just a job; it was a way of life. I decided to stay and work for what I thought was fair and right.

Plain and simple: I was too invested emotionally into Palmer & Cay. I still held out hope that I would not be going down with The Ship.

Part III

The Third Year
(January–May 2005)

Chapter 38

Company Spiraling out of Control

By the year's end, things were pretty sad: The numbers were awful, we were not meeting the loan covenants, people were leaving, the outside world was starting to take notice, and those close to the center were spending more time talking about the problems than selling and servicing customers. Still, some people persisted in claiming that everything was good. During one of the sales meetings hosted by Mike Liss, Jim Meathe stepped in for a few words. When asked about how the year was going to end, he replied, "Break even, or possibly a little better."

I just sat there in disbelief. I knew the numbers and was sure he was misleading us. I looked over at Mike, but he would not make eye contact.

One quiet morning, I was sitting in Mike's office having a social conversation when Fran Millar bounded in, all upbeat. "Just had a talk with Jim! I think everything is going to be okay."

"What makes you think so?" I asked.

"Jim said things are turning around."

"Did he give you any numbers?" I responded.

"No."

"Then you have nothing, no clue, nothing." Fran was taken aback by the tone of my verbal attack. "In fact, you have no idea what's going on without any numbers."

I would not let it go, and Fran was getting worked up. "I will go ask him." With that, he wheeled around and flew out the door.

From behind his desk, I heard Mike's raspy voice: "Jesus, you were hard on him," followed by hearty laughter.

"I am tired of all the bullshit!" Mike and I both knew the numbers and how grave the situation had become. Fran came back a few minutes later and said that Jim told him he would be releasing numbers soon. We all knew that was not going to happen, so I just gave it a rest.

Then Ron Norelli, an independent business consultant sent by Wachovia, showed up at our door to review the company. John claimed that he requested a fresh look at the company, but we all felt that it was really Wachovia directing this action. My guess is the bank wanted to evaluate the real story without the smoke screen from the Meathe administration. Wachovia had loaned Palmer & Cay around $60 million, but I believed that their real motivation was to buy us cheap. Our financial troubles would make it easier for them to take over the company without spending big bucks.

Let me lay out the background. In recent years, the big banks had been buying up the insurance-brokerage firms to fill out their financial-services offerings. Once one bank announced their plans, the other banks followed in line, not wanting to miss out on what they perceived as a sound business move. This was taking place all over the country. Wells Fargo had an insurance division, Wachovia had previously bought a firm in Atlanta known as HDA, and BB&T had recently purchased McGriff Seibel. Rumor had it that both HDA and McGriff sold for two and a half to three times revenue, exorbitant prices for the insurance-brokerage business.

Our competitors were individually becoming rich. In the case of HDA, they were first purchased by Wachovia at a healthy price and then, when Wachovia was purchased by First Union, they got more money plus a bonus: their change-of-control agreement kicked in and they were free to take their profits and cash out. At McGriff, management decided that after paying out all the shareholders they would distribute around $12 million of the remaining dollars to all the employees. Both of these firms hit the market just right.

This is what I had hoped for Palmer & Cay. Instead, we were all worried about losing everything. Everyone, that is, except for the three geniuses who had put us in this precarious position. They each would get $5 million, no matter what.

One day when entering our office building, I ran into Will Underwood in the elevator lobby. Will was the salesman who most actively embraced the new regime and had become close friends with the national sales manager, Bill Lenhart. When we started talking about the state of the company, things became heated quickly. We talked in halted speech on the ride up so not to cause a scene in front of the noncompany people sharing the elevator. It was clear we were on different sides of the company's problems. I purposely passed up my floor to stay with Will so we could continue our conversation. When we got off the elevator together, Will turned to me and in an angry voice said, "Ron, this is the way the company is going, and I don't hear negative talk when I travel around the other offices. Most people don't feel like you do, and it could be bad for your career if you don't change your attitude."

With that, he stormed away. I was left there thinking, *We are about to lose the whole company and he thinks it is about company politics.* From that encounter, I learned not to share what I knew, with few exceptions. However, I was certain that the end of Palmer & Cay was near.

The newly hired Atlanta manager, Mike Liss, had similar thoughts. One morning while sitting in his office, just the two of us, he confided that he fessed up last night to his wife about the company's state of affairs. I had wondered when he would have that conversation, since she had been dead set against his joining Palmer & Cay and moving from Chicago to Atlanta.

"What did she say? How did she react?" I questioned.

"She went ballistic. She wanted to hit me on my bald head."

I believed him. I had only met her once, from what I could recall, and that was the night we were selling them on Atlanta. From my conversations with Mike, I knew her to be a tough, scrappy woman. They had turned their whole lives upside down just a few months prior, and now everything was falling apart. Mike's family had not assimilated very well in the short time they had been in town, neither wife nor children. There would be many more uncomfortable discussions ahead for the associates and families of Palmer & Cay.

* * *

As part of his review of Palmer & Cay, Ron Norelli conducted a series of interviews with some of the senior managers. When it was my turn, we talked about the goings-on of the benefits area and the company as a whole. When I mentioned that the company was in "dire straits," he interrupted me to defend the company as not being in that bad of shape. When I pointed out we were $60 million in debt, not meeting loan covenants, fighting lawsuits, and losing accounts with no offsetting increase in revenue, he put his hand on his forehead, looked down, and said, "I guess dire straits is right."

* * *

Two events would soon come together to really get the rumors flowing. First, John Cay announced he was asking his wife for a divorce, and then Stephens, Inc., a financial-service firm out of Arkansas, was hired by Palmer & Cay. Stephens is a well-known, prestigious, private banking company with a national reputation. They were known as the financial force behind Walmart way back when, and also helped raise money for the Louisiana Superdome after Wall Street refused the project. Everyone speculated that John Cay was putting the company up for sale to fund his divorce. I knew better. The two things were coincidental. We just could not financially afford to continue; we were in trouble. I am sure that the bank was also exerting pressure for action to avoid a total loss. Because we were both old Southern firms, we were very familiar with the people at Stephens, and them with us. Once Stephens began to talk with potential suitors, the word would leak out that we were for sale.

Chapter 39

Changes in Attitude

Walking into the reception area one afternoon, I found Fran Millar sprawled out on the sofa and Phil Maddox standing nearby. I asked, "What's up, guys?"

Phil responded, "Fran talked with his lawyer."

"What did he say?" I asked. I had been hoping someone would seek legal advice about the rights of the minority shareholders. Fran was the perfect person for this task, as he had already sued a former employer and, as I previously pointed out, won big. We all knew his law firm was very good and not afraid of a fight.

"He said stupidity is not illegal!" Fran responded with a look of disgust on his face.

"Yeah, it seems that it is not against the law to be dumb," chimed in Phil.

How disappointing! We had to take the lawyer's word for the fact we had no case; however, I could not help hoping that we would have some grounds to go after the people who had changed our company. Looking back, I wish I had investigated for myself whether I had any legal rights.

* * *

It was around this time that I noticed a change in people's attitudes toward the company. While everyone recognized that it was the new management's mistakes that put us in this bind, the anger was being directed at John Cay for sitting back and letting it happen. As Jeannie said, "What is John doing about it? He is the one who brought these people in."

Jim Meathe, at times, came across as an affable, friendly person, and Mike Liss was very likable. Plus, Mike was not at fault for any company decisions since he only ran the Atlanta office. Actually, Mike recognized the need for better morale and decided to take action. He called for a quarterly meeting of the Atlanta office to be held in a nearby hotel ballroom. The place was packed; I guess everyone wanted to see what it was about. Mike asked me to take part in two ways: First, to lead a discussion on new things we were implementing to increase sales, and second, to give out some awards in recognition of individual performance. The sales part of the meeting did not go well. The salespeople did not respond. I threw out suggestions, but no one spoke. I asked questions, but no one answered. They were no longer believers; they just sat there.

The awards presentation was entirely different. Mike had picked four people to receive a few hundred-dollar bills and I was to say something nice about each one. I started with an actuary named Clinton. Unfortunately, he was not there, but I went on with my prepared remarks for the crowd. In the insurance business, actuaries are often the butt of jokes, and I was ready with mine. Clinton had been in the military as a controller for the Patriot-guided missile, so one of my punchlines was "What was the military thinking, putting a weapon of mass destruction in the hands of an actuary?" That softened up the crowd and got them in a better mood. One of the other recipients was Fran Millar's account manager, Rene. Before I said her name, I started out by saying, "The one thing everyone wants to know about our next award winner is, How does she work for that guy? He is loud, aggressive, demanding, and somewhat pushy." Then I introduced Rene. She came up front to receive her envelope and gave me a big hug.

As Rene went back to her seat, I made a big production about going over my notes while whispering out loud so everyone could hear me, "Loud, aggressive, demanding, and pushy." Then I folded that piece of paper and, while putting it into my pocket, I said, "I better keep these notes because someday I may be asked to introduce Sue (Meathe's assistant)." Everyone burst out laughing. I looked over at Jim Meathe, who was surrounded by a number of his guys who were all hooting and cracking up. Jim raised his arm and pointed his finger at me, but all that came out of his mouth was "You, you, you." He was also laughing hard. I remember thinking he was not a bad guy, and under different circumstances he would have been fun to hang with. Unfortunately, before it was all over, he would end up costing me over a million dollars in the current and future value of the company. Jim's management of the company would be the sole reason all my plans for a comfortable retirement would be dashed. At my age, this was a cruel turn of events.

Also around this time, I became acquainted with a specialist from one of the Midwest offices who worked exclusively with architectural and engineering firms. She traveled to Atlanta often to work with a client that was one of the best-known architectural firms in the country. It just so happened that the president of the firm was a good friend of mine. Therefore, by extension, this consultant and I also became friends.

One day when our conversation focused on Palmer & Cay and its leadership, she gave me an insight into Jim Meathe's family that may have been a clue to his behavior. She informed me that Jim's father had been the president of an architectural firm in Detroit and somewhat of an important figure in the community. Although the firm had a boardroom named after Jim's father, there was no fondness for him within the organization. Evidently, he had been difficult to work with. Was Jim emulating his father? Was he trying to prove himself to Dad? Or was he just a chip off the block? I don't know enough to say, but he was certainly a different leader than what we wanted or needed.

* * *

Everyone had waited for almost two years for John to take control back from the outsiders, and had now lost patience with the situation. So why didn't John take control? After all, he had been telling people that Jim Meathe was acting reckless in his management of the company.

One day I found him alone in his office and asked him to lunch. We walked to a nearby sandwich shop and sat outdoors for a quick bite. Sitting at a table on Piedmont Road, I asked him why he didn't just sell the company while it was still worth something. He did not respond to my question, maybe thinking it was more of a rhetorical statement. My best guess is that John did not want to pay the $15 million that it would have cost to rid ourselves of the three people responsible for creating the disaster. He probably found it difficult to think in terms of $15 million out the door immediately versus the unknown loss of value sometime later, which could not be measured in the present. Writing three $5-million checks for basically no value would have been hard for John. Other companies in similar situations had reversed course and survived, but John could not pull the trigger on such a dramatic move. He was like a gambler on a losing streak who just could not walk away from the tables, too far in to quit.

It had occurred to me that maybe it was John's small-town background that caused his paralysis in dealing with the company troubles. Growing up and starting his business career in Savannah, John's small-town values included honoring contracts, working hard, and persevering through trial and error. He insisted on fulfilling his side of the agreement while the new management was willing to destroy his life's work. His other option, as I have mentioned before, would have been to pay the $15 million and regroup from there. That, too, would have gone against his small-town roots. Unfortunately, that $15 million would have been a lot less than what we ended up losing in the value of the company.

Chapter 40

The Godfather Call

As discontent and worry increased, an informal network of information gatherers (spies) was formed. This group included individuals from several Palmer & Cay offices, not just Atlanta. Somehow, perhaps because of our long history together, people just seemed to know who was in the know and who could be trusted. The extent of this underground system was revealed to me unexpectedly in the form of a phone number in Savannah. Directions were to call the number and punch in the code to retrieve messages. I was a little worried about participating in this clandestine activity. Up to that point, my actions had been confined to looking at reports that management did not want me to see, mostly provided to me by John Cay. Yet that evening after everyone near me had left for the day, I closed my door and made the call. As soon as the recording began, I wished I had never dialed the number. However, that feeling of regret did not stop me from listening to the whole message.

I was so rattled that I cannot remember if the voice said "John" or "Johnny," but it was clearly someone talking down to John Cay as if he were a child. The voice was husky with a slow, deliberate cadence. There was the heavy breathing that comes from a man with a wide girth. It was board member Joe Platt playing the role of a movie heavy, figuratively and literally. It was really disconcerting to hear the chairman, the leader of our company, talked to in such fashion. Evidentially, Joe must have gotten wind of something that John was changing his mind about, and this call was to bring him back in line. Whatever it was, Joe was letting John know that he needed to follow through like they had agreed when they last met. The tone was almost like "We gave you your orders, and you need to see them through."

I was so stunned, I didn't think to make notes of the exact words. What was so galling was that this person, who had only recently appeared on the scene, who did not have an office at Palmer & Cay, and whose direction as a board member was keeping many of us up at night, had the nerve to address John in this manner. John, on the other hand, had provided the vision and hard work to get us where we were before the outsiders showed up. He spent twelve-hour days for years concentrating solely on the company. He didn't do it by himself, but no one worked any harder or contributed more to the company than John Cay.

Prior to that phone message, when I asked what Gussenhoven and Platt were doing for the company, I was always told that they were working on the outside helping recruit people and helping to establish relationships, whatever that meant. After that call, I quit asking.

Chapter 41

My Problems Continue

My relationship with Ray Slabaugh and Dave Morgan continued to deteriorate. I was not happy about the lack of support my office was receiving from Richmond and the too-frequent interference from Ray into Atlanta business. In turn, they were not happy about something I had said to an outsider a long time ago about the business practices of certain people on Ray's staff. Those comments kept coming back to haunt me. I sought counsel from Frank Beard, who suggested I get on an airplane and go to Richmond to work things out. Taking his advice, I placed a call to Dave to set up a meeting. Something must have triggered a new round of anger because not only were they agreeable to a meeting, they demanded I come up that Friday, only a few days away. And they let me know I was in for a rough time.

Thinking it over, I decided that I would not go to Richmond just for a confrontation. It sounded to me like they had no intention

of working out an amicable plan for getting along. I called Dave
back to tell him that the coming weekend was my anniversary and
I would be spending it with my wife in Atlanta. He was not
happy, but there was nothing he could do; I was not going to
Richmond.

I then went back upstairs to let Frank know what had transpired.
He was stunned. "What do you mean, you are not going? They
ordered you to show up."

I responded, "I'm not going. Let them fire me."

Frank, a former sailor, was still thinking in old-school terms
of employer-employee relationships, hence his shock that I
would disobey a direct order from above. In all fairness, he had
not yet adjusted to the new reality of Palmer & Cay. I had never
viewed Ray or Dave as my peers, much less my bosses. The
company was on the verge of collapse, we were on the market to
be sold, and everyone was busy taking care of their own issues.
Had Ray or Dave tried to fire me, they would have looked silly,
and neither the old nor the new management would have
allowed it. The last thing the company needed was a major
disruption of the flagship office in the flagship benefits department.

Was I the only one who knew the end was near? I doubt it.
Maybe I was one of the first to face the reality while others chose
to not to come to terms with the situation. Many just did not have
enough information to come to the realization I had. Others may
have thought the company would always be there and never gave
it another minute of consideration. Many were in for a rude
awakening.

On the other hand, Ray Slabaugh by now had fully transi-
tioned to the Meathe team. He saw John as the weak former
leader and Jim as fully in control. This was his opportunity to
improve his standing in the company. Ray could be heard
backing Jim at every chance. Once again, he took in all the

information and came to the conclusion he, Ray, wanted rather than what was the real circumstance. He made no attempt to hide his feelings from those of us who saw things differently. I wondered if he really thought Jim Meathe would survive a change in ownership.

Chapter 42

Palmer & Cay for Sale

Once Stephens, Inc. became involved, the universal assumption was that the company was for sale. At first, there was a great deal of interest. To the outside world, we still had a pristine reputation, the largest footprint of any independent in the Southeast, a great client list, and many highly skilled professionals. Unfortunately, along with all those good attributes came $60 million of debt, which represented over 40 percent of our annual revenues. Not good for a financial-services firm of our size. Also, we had a number of fully staffed offices with little revenue flowing in. Stephens put together a package for the offering.

After we got past the initial round of interest, it became apparent to all that our great little company was no longer the valuable asset it once had been. Wachovia was sitting outside the door waiting to pounce on the remains at a significant discount. Two years prior, with $135 million in revenue, Palmer & Cay would have sold for between $270 million and $405 million based on multiples at the time. The banks were buying commercial insurance brokers anywhere from two to three times revenue. That was for well-run firms with low-debt ratios, which Palmer and Cay had been. As the second-largest independent in the country, we would have sold for a premium. Now we were generating a lot of interest until potential buyers took a closer look and punted. It was not just the debt, but all the overpaid, overstaffed offices that were not producing revenue.

One day, in a conversation with the young lady who had been in Christopher Cay's wedding, she volunteered that her father worked for an investment company and she could see if they were interested. It felt really strange, talking to someone who worked for me about this problem, especially someone half my age. I told her to go ahead. Several days later, she reported back that her father said they had already seen the package from Stephens and there just was too much debt for them. It really hurt my pride to hear this feedback. Palmer & Cay was no longer special. The magic was gone.

In a conversation with Mike Liss, I asked him what, if anything, he had heard from Jim Meathe. Jim had become scarce around the Atlanta office. With an office on a lower floor, we just never saw him. What I understood from administrative people was that he was out often. In his usual direct and honest manner, Mike said he had talked with Jim and that Jim was embarrassed. Jim had never failed at anything before, and he was struggling with what had happened to the company. "Humiliated" is the word he used.

Phil Maddox was especially unhappy because he was planning on retiring soon with a nice pot of cash, much of which was tied to Palmer & Cay stock. Phil had joined Palmer & Cay several years before me when he sold his business to the company. He had been instrumental in introducing John Cay to many people in the Atlanta business and social communities. I am sure he felt that his was a special situation that John should treat accordingly. Word got back to me that Phil had gone to John Cay and asked that he make good on whatever Phil would lose as a result of the company problems. John turned him down. John took a social hit for that, since Phil had become president of the Piedmont Driving Club, the most exclusive social club in Atlanta, where word could easily be spread. Phil was already disgruntled, and he knew every player in the Atlanta social scene, including the richest man in Georgia and all his friends. He was the one person in the organization who really could sink John's reputation. Even when John was away from Atlanta, he could not escape Phil's eye. I walked into Phil's office one day and he was quick to tell me that John had tried to jump ahead of a crowd for a table in a posh restaurant in Charleston over the weekend. To hear Phil tell the story, John was arrogantly incredulous that they wouldn't seat him right away. I am sure I was not the only one to hear that story.

Things were looking pretty grim. Wachovia's first offer was insulting. After taking money out to pay off our debt, we probably would not even get one times annual revenue, or around $140 million. Anyone who had a clue was incredibly stressed out. It was surreal. Those in management at a senior level could not sleep at night from worry, and those on the day-to-day working level went about their business oblivious to what lay ahead. To many, this was a nightmare that could not possibly have been happening to us. We were not some company you read about in the business section that failed due to mismanagement. That wasn't supposed to happen to Palmer & Cay; we were too good. We were special—or had been.

Chapter 43

A White Knight

Things were getting desperate; we could not go on much longer. John Cay was reaching out to anyone who showed any interest in purchasing the company. I could not look at John without seeing worry on his face. We needed someone else to help create a market, or Wachovia would pick us clean. One night, John was in New York having dinner with some people from a London insurance broker. As luck would have it, also dining in the same restaurant that evening was Joe Plumeri, chairman of Willis, the third-largest national insurance-brokerage firm in the US. Joe was a well-known figure in the industry. He was the aggressive leader who turned Willis into a major player, mostly through acquisitions. When Joe saw John sitting with the guys from London, it did not take him long to figure out what was going on. Plus, by now he had probably heard the rumors about Palmer & Cay's problems.

The next day John was back in his office in Savannah when his secretary announced that a Mister Plumeri was on the phone. Joe came right to the point: He had seen John the evening before in New York with the Brits, and if he was selling the company, Joe wanted to buy. Joe's first offer must have caused heartburn in Charlotte at Wachovia's home office. Finally, a real offer was on the table. This would begin a back-and-forth bidding for Palmer & Cay.

It was around this time that another large insurance-brokerage firm with plenty of money also took an interest in Palmer & Cay. The firm went by the initials of HRH and was headquartered in Richmond. This must have been disconcerting to John Cay, since the president of HRH was Mike Crowley. As in the Karen Lehman story, a former executive whom John bypassed was coming back to haunt him. If HRH were to buy Palmer & Cay, would John be working for Mike? A number of people wondered out loud about that possibility. At this point, the one thing I was sure of was that John would not sell the company to HRH unless he was truly desperate.

It was clear now that the company would at least have options instead of a railroaded deal from the bank. John began asking people which way he should go—the bank or the insurance broker? When asked, I mistakenly said the bank. I knew what they had done for my competitor HDA in driving business their way, and I wanted a share of the business. Plus, I wanted to feel what it would be like to walk into a prospect's office for once knowing there was a higher power behind me. Also, I knew that John favored the bank from the time he served on the board of a Savannah-based bank that became part of First Union. What I didn't take into consideration was what it would be like working for a bank. Banks have a totally different culture than that of an entrepreneurial insurance broker. As I was talking with John, I had no concept of the internal workings of a large bank. I had a lot to learn.

Every time Wachovia raised their offer, Willis (Plumeri's company) increased their offer and terms. Eventually it came down to whom we wanted to dance with.

While all this was going on, John finally made the decision to remove Meathe from the presidency. He gave the board no choice in the matter. During the restructuring of the stock, John created super shares for himself that gave him ultimate control of the company. Now he was voting his stock. When John went to Jim and announced his decision, Jim defiantly replied that he couldn't do that since he had a contract. John replied he was not being fired, just demoted. And to make matters even more embarrassing for Jim, the new president would be John's thirty-something son Jack Cay.

This was more than Jim could handle. From then on, he let everyone know he would be working from home. While Jim cooled his heels, Jack Cay traveled to the offices to be introduced as the new president. I'm not sure why we were going through with this charade, as it was clear that his tenure would be short lived. As soon as a sale went through, we would be under new management. One morning, I heard John on the telephone telling someone that he had installed Jack as the president, thus continuing the line of Cays at the top, totally ignoring the fact that we were losing the company.

Chapter 44

Taking on Water

To our benefit, the competition continued between Wachovia and Willis. I could not prove it, but I knew John was favoring Wachovia and, therefore, informally helping them meet each Willis offer. While all this was going on, some of us were still trying to be in the insurance business. Not surprisingly, it became increasingly harder as each day went by with the Sword of Damocles hanging over our heads.

One project that I had been working on was to bring in a new, large client. Like many large accounts, this had been a multiple-year effort. The company was headquartered in Atlanta with plants in multiple states. They had around five thousand employees, which, for an Atlanta company, made them a big group-insurance account. The commissions would be in the hundreds of thousands of dollars per year. This was a privately held company in the package-printing business. Many well-known consumer products were packaged with materials that had been through their plants.

The owners were closely tied to Georgia Tech and well known in the Atlanta business and social communities.

While serving on various committees of The Southern Employee Benefits Conference, I had gotten to know the CFO of this printing company. Over time at different meetings and social gatherings, we had become casual business friends. At the time, they were using a captive insurance agency owned in part by the family that owned the printing company. A determination was made that the company had outgrown the services of the current group, and they would take bids from some of the bigger firms in Atlanta. I felt really good about our chances for a number of reasons. First, we knew the CFO, which in most firms gives you a strong ally. Second, in the last year we had hired a friend of mine who also knew the CFO, and they had been friends for around thirty years. And finally, and maybe most importantly, Palmer & Cay was a local Southern firm with a great reputation. We were already doing business with many of the largest high-profile companies in Atlanta, Georgia, and the Southeast. I could tell from talking with Mike, their CFO, that they were not necessarily enthralled with working with the big national firms.

After putting a team together, we pulled out all stops to respond to the specifications that went out to the insurance-brokerage companies included on the bid list. This was the kind of work we were really good at, and we had the resources to look good in the beauty-contest part of the process. The date and time was set for our finalist meeting with the prospect; we were ready for show time. There was only one problem that had me concerned: it was about to be announced that Palmer & Cay was being purchased by Wachovia. The only thing I could do was face the truth and hope they would understand.

On the appointed day, we showed up with a team of polished insurance professionals. In the meeting from the prospect side was the CFO, the head of HR, someone from administration, and one or two others that I don't recall. We started with introductions. I introduced my team and Mike, the CFO, introduced his people. Then, before getting into the meat of the presentation, Mike said he had something he wanted to say. They had heard a rumor that Palmer & Cay was up for sale. I responded that yes, it was true, and in fact there would be an announcement shortly stating we were being purchased by Wachovia. I could tell by the looks on their faces that we were dead on arrival. There was no chance we would win this contest. I could barely go through the motions. I tried to explain that even though we were being purchased, those of us in the room would still be working on behalf of our clients.

A week later I got the call. "Ron, it's Mike."

"Hello, Mike, it's good to hear from you."

"Listen, this call is in follow-up to our meeting last week. Our committee has met with all the bidders and made a decision. I wanted to personally call you first, and then I will give John Cay a call to tell him the same thing. We have decided not to choose Palmer & Cay. We know where you're going with this sale. We have seen this before and just don't want to be part of it. I know it is no consolation; however, had it not been for this news of the sale, you would have been picked as our broker. We were really impressed with your team."

With that phone call, it was all over. Two years of patience and waiting down the drain. It should have been our account. You don't get many chances at the big ones; they don't change hands often, and this one was meant for us.

While I was going through my disappointment, Mike Liss was facing a similar situation on the commercial-insurance side. Same scenario, different prospect. I walked into his office right after he got the bad news, and he was fuming. "We are not even winning the ones we are supposed to get!" While commiserating, we decided to have lunch later in the week. We chose the Atlanta Fish Market on Pharr Road. We started with martinis and drank until we had a buzz. Then we proceeded to eat until we sobered up, which required us to go through over two hundred dollars for lunch. What the heck. I would submit the expense and he would approve it. That was the only time we did anything like that, and we felt we were deserving.

Chapter 45

Going Under

Once the word got out that Wachovia was buying Palmer & Cay, a number of interesting things occurred. First, I almost immediately received a call from an in-house recruiter with Willis in New York, who was quick to remind me that he had called me the year before. I figured he mentioned that conversation because as part of the bidding process, the loser is not supposed to go back and recruit employees when their bid is not chosen. He could claim ours was a continuing conversation started before the bidding. I told him I was not interested. What I didn't say was that I was spent, that I could no longer fight the corporate battles.

Another day I had a welcome surprise visitor. Karen Lehman, our former CFO whom Jim Meathe had run off almost immediately when joining the company, was now the CFO of Wachovia's insurance services in Charlotte. She and her boss were in town ahead of the formal acquisition. You could not wipe the smile off her face. Talk about a turnaround. In less than two years, she was in a position of payback to both Jim Meathe and John Cay. Any valuation of the purchase price would have to go through her calculations, and she was good at her job. There would be no spare change in the final accounting of this deal. For now, she was going to get the satisfaction of an office tour as the conqueror, and I would be the guide. When we went downstairs, I told her not to worry about running into Jim, as he no longer came into the office.

After the acquisition was final, I learned of an interesting incident that happened just before the closing. I was told that our in-house corporate attorney, David Hofele, was presenting a stack of documents for John Cay to sign as part of the transaction. When John came to one document that he did not recognize, he asked David to explain. It was a guarantee of one year's compensation for David. As tight as John could be with money, I can imagine his reaction. David explained that once the deal closed, he would be out of a job and this was for all the work he was expected to do beforehand. In other words, if John wanted his help, he needed to sign this guarantee, which he did. That must have been a bittersweet moment for David since he had feelings about John's treatment of him. David was hired as a young attorney, and John probably always viewed him as such. The workload was heavy, and help was not forthcoming until the new management took charge.

Before the closing, everyone from Wachovia was very friendly. There were some preliminary gatherings including visits with some of the executives at the Wachovia Insurance Services office in Atlanta. There was talk about how the offices would be integrated. I spoke with Frank Beard about my role in the whole process since he had been through this same situation three or four years earlier at another company. He just shook his head and said, "That's not how this will work." I would basically have no say in anything. I was still under the misconception that the new company would evaluate talent and figure out who was best positioned for each management job. I had won multiple national awards at one of the largest companies in the insurance business and had built the Palmer & Cay benefits operation into one of the largest and best in Atlanta. I was feeling pretty good about myself. How naïve I was! Performance and track record had nothing to do with anything going on at Wachovia. They didn't want to know.

* * *

The nightmare had lasted for almost two years, and this would be as close as we would get to waking up from a bad dream. After two years of drama and a fair amount of stress, it was finally over. Ironically, the end came on a bright, beautiful, clear-blue-sky spring day, as if to signal the storm had passed. That morning I was talking with one of our consultants, Bill Danish, and I said, "The last shareholder meeting is upstairs in the conference room. Let's go see what it is about."

His answer: "Sure, why not?"

As I sat with my back to the windows, observing the calm through the glass dividing wall between the conference room and reception area, my thoughts contrasted how different things were from when we moved to this office space six years earlier. I remember telling anyone who would listen that they were building my last office in the insurance business. When we took over the top floor of this new office tower, we were a bright, energetic, high-achieving group of people. We were now in an upscale part of town, and our offices were in a new building that still smelled of fresh concrete. The main reception area was handsomely appointed with dark-wood walls, carefully selected Persian rugs, and traditional furnishings. The look was more of a midsize law firm than that of an insurance brokerage. We were very proud of our surroundings and our company.

Until recently, the reception area and adjoining, glass-enclosed, board-style conference room had been the center of activity. The receptionist was constantly answering the phone, greeting visitors, or accepting deliveries. People hustled through, meeting and greeting as they passed. Everyone carried themselves with the confidence that comes with knowing you are successful. Clients and vendors were glad to be seen with us. Potential employees coming in for interviews were on their best behavior, looking sharp and keenly focused.

Where did all the people go? What happened to all the activity? Having observed the ups and downs of companies for thirty-plus years, one thing I find interesting is how a company can be gauged by the attendance of its people. When things are positive, people arrive at work early, stay late, and often come in after hours, especially on weekends. When things are not going so well, people seem to find somewhere else to spend their time. In our case, that change had occurred months ago. The halls were quiet now, the break rooms empty, and the phones not so busy. Some people had left the company, but most were just keeping a low profile, staying out of the office for any number of reasons, real or made up. Some were out looking for new jobs.

Without people traffic, one easily notices the failing physical condition of a company. Everything somehow seems grayer, more dilapidated. The office space could use refreshing, but the people normally in charge of upkeep were no longer around. For months, no one had cared about the routine tasks. We were no longer proud. Becoming part of a bank was depressing. What would become of the two etched-glass panels in the conference-room doors? Each side of the double doors had glass that displayed the company logo, the SS *Savannah*, the first steamship to cross the Atlantic. The way you could tell it was the *Savannah* was the bent smokestack between the first and second mast. Besides a classy symbol, the ship was very apropos, consistent with our headquarter city and our early roots in the marine-insurance business. At a time when others were adopting logos from made-up names, abbreviations, or modern art, Palmer & Cay had a standard that represented something substantial with historical significance.

On this glorious day, Bill, Fran Millar, and I, along with only a handful of the twelve hundred associates, witnessed the last (my first and only) shareholder meeting of the 137-year-old company. A meeting that would effectively be the end of a company that less than twenty-four months earlier was the toast of the insurance industry. A meeting unattended by the major players responsible for one of the quickest downfalls in American business.

And why have you not heard this story? The answer, unfortunately, is that at $148 million in revenue, with twelve hundred associates in twenty-eight offices in twelve states, we were simply too small to receive any news coverage. All the outside world knew was that Palmer & Cay was being purchased by a big bank, which was what was happening to many firms during this period of consolidation in the insurance-brokerage community. An ironic fact is that even our closest friends had no idea of the trauma we were all suffering. Our clients and vendors still viewed us as the successful company that we once were, and to make matters worse, many people thought we were getting rich, like so many others had, by selling out to the banks or larger competitors. This story, nonetheless, is still worth knowing, as it may be seen as a foreboding of what would hit the entire country three years later. No doubt, the lessons learned will be repeated at some future date, as it is human nature to forget past mistakes and start a new cycle of folly.

David led John through the formality of the shareholders meeting until right before the end, when the sale of Palmer & Cay would receive shareholder approval. John, sitting at the head of the conference table with a portrait of his father, golf club in hand, staring down at him, asked for our indulgence while he spoke a few words. What followed was a journey through the history of the company, with John finishing by wondering what his father might think of these events were he around to witness this day. I am sure that we were all wondering something similar. Would his father be proud of John's accomplishment of growing a single-office insurance agency of $3 million into a multistate company with close to $150 million of revenue? Or would he focus on the failure of the last two years?

John was so melancholy, I wondered if the Cays weren't Irish instead of British. When John was through speaking, we all casually shuffled out of the room.

Palmer & Cay was no more.

Chapter 46

The Aftermath

There is often a significant difference between being a prospective employee and being an actual employee. Sort of like going from being a prospect to being a client. This concept was no truer than at Wachovia. As the saying goes, "No more Mr. Nice Guy." This was the first time I experienced this change in attitude at a senior-management level. Earlier in my career I was with a company that was purchased twice; however, I was a junior person well below the radar and therefore knew nothing of what transpired above me.

At first it was the little things, like having to pay for your own lunch when traveling to Charlotte for meetings you were required to attend. Then there was the lack of communications; no one wanted to hear from you. And, finally, there was a sales meeting in Atlanta that included an outing at Turner Field for a Braves baseball game. That one was particularly hard for me, as I might as well have been invisible. I had been senior management for the last sixteen years, and the Wachovia management just looked right through me. It was that night in a conversation with one of my former consultants that I first said I didn't think I could stick around. I meant not only that night, but going forward with the company.

A phone call from an HR contact shed some light on my future. From that conversation, I learned two things that had not been publicized. First, the bank had a personnel policy that said no existing employee could lose his or her position due to an acquisition. Since Wachovia Insurance Services already had an office in Atlanta and there was already someone heading up the benefits department, I would not be allowed to compete for the job. Talent, background, ability, and accomplishments would not be factored. This was just the kind of thinking that caused me and many others to leave the big firms for the freedom and opportunities an entrepreneurial organization offered. Decisions were not being made based on what was best for clients, employees, or even the corporation itself. In fact, when the reorganization was announced, the senior management for the entire region, including Atlanta, was filled based on diversity with no regard to qualifications. Our region was turned over to a very nice man who had only been in the insurance business for a short while and only on the insurance-company side. He had no clue about the world of insurance brokers.

The second thing I learned was that if I handled the situation in a certain manner, I could get a termination package, hopefully at my level of a year's pay. Knowing this, I was able to make my next move when the time was right. I didn't have to wait long. The call, when it came, was interesting in itself. Here I was, a senior officer with one of the largest and most profitable operations in the company, and I got a call from a secretary to set up an interview with the manager of the combined Atlanta offices.

That part was fine—many people on the executive level don't set up their own appointments. What was off-putting was when I asked how long I should schedule the meeting for, to which she replied, "Fifteen minutes should be fine." Fifteen minutes to discuss my future with the company! I had given so much time to this job, both during regular hours and many outside hours, and now they were giving me fifteen minutes. Adding to the insult, she informed me that the man I should be competing with would also be in the interview. My contact in HR was right. The decisions had already been made, and I would no longer be in management.

At the designated time, the two men showed up at my office and we closed the door for our discussion. Gone was all the warmth and comradery of the previous weeks leading up to the closing. It was obvious this would be uncomfortable for them, and I was not about to make it easier. Basically, their only question was what I wanted to do going forward. They really didn't want to know anything about me or how I could best help the company. Stealing a line from John Cay, I said we had been so successful at Palmer & Cay that I wanted to see how far we could go together with me leading the combined benefits operation. They had looks on their faces as if someone farted. Looking back on it now, it was comical. However, at the time, I was so pissed off at the lack of respect that I was really digging in. I wanted the termination package but knew better than to bring it up. I wanted them to think I was a problem that could not be solved. We did not even use up the allotted fifteen minutes. When they left, I was sure my time had run its course.

It did not take long; they acted quickly. Within days, I got a message to meet in Mike Liss's office. Mike was still head of the Palmer & Cay section of the Atlanta operation. When I walked into his office, I found an HR person with him and a large, thick envelope in front of Mike on his desk. There was no need for much of a discussion, and I had no problem with Mike. He explained that I was getting a six-month package, to which I replied that I thought as a senior vice president/managing partner with sixteen years of service, I should have been given one month per year, or at least one full year of income. That is when I was introduced to the term "mapping." Evidently, some committee at the bank sat down and determined what titles from Palmer & Cay translated to in bank titles. As commonly known, banks give away titles in lieu of actual compensation. Officer's titles are basically worthless from the bank's point of view. There was no reason for the mapping committee to be generous; in fact, there may have even been some resentment in their collective thinking. I could not get out of there quickly enough.

It did not take long for the word to get out. Before I could clear out of my office, the calls started coming in.

Frank Beard first: "No job, no job, no job," he kept repeating.

"Frank, it's all right," I said. "This is what I wanted. I got a package and can get out of here."

John Cay: "Now Ron, why don't you stay and work with us in sales? I can talk with Wachovia, and I'm sure we can work out something."

"John, I want out, but you can help me," I said. "I am disappointed that my package is only for six months after all I have contributed."

John said he would see what he could do.

Ray Slabaugh called wanting to know the details. I made the mistake of telling him about the package. He did not know that was an option. As I mentioned before, the bank kept package deals hush-hush. Later, I would learn from Ian Robb that Ray was going around telling everyone who would listen he got a package for a year. Of course, this caused HR all kinds of headaches. To this day, I am not sure he got anything. Ray was already past bank-retirement age, and they did not have to give him anything. Ray being Ray, it was always hard to know what was true.

Jack Cay called and wanted to get together. We met at a bakery on Piedmont Road for coffee. Since he was, for the time being, still president of Palmer & Cay, he was making an effort in talking me into staying with the company. It was a short, pleasant, but unproductive meeting.

Chapter 47

Goodbye, Palmer & Cay

The end, when it came for me, was quick and unceremonious. My staff organized an after-work get-together at the Rock Bottom Brewery, which was our main go-to place in good times. The group was made up primarily of our people on the twelfth floor. There may have been a few others, but I was too emotional to make note of everyone. There were a few short speeches, but I did not have much to say. We mostly just hung out as we had done many times before. I had hired almost everyone there, and we were a great working team and friends on a personal level.

As I looked around the room, I could not help but feel like I was being robbed of the psychological reward that should come with my position in life. I had been planning on retiring in five or six years. My plan had been that after growing the business to whatever level we could achieve, I would help select my successor and groom that person to take over. At the appropriate time, the company would throw me a retirement dinner and, with my family by my side, I could ride off into the sunset knowing I was leaving something behind that was substantial and sustainable.

That opportunity was lost to me.

At my age, there was no time left for another twenty-year career. Anyway, I'm not sure I would have had the energy to do it all over again.

* * *

Palmer & Cay was ahead of the times! Several years after the Palmer & Cay debacle, the United States, along with the rest of the world, was thrown into financial crisis. The chaos was precipitated by the mortgage industry in the United States deciding to shortcut the loan-approval process for buying homes by ignoring tried-and-tested underwriting guidelines. Thousands and thousands of people with or without jobs or income were given home loans. During that period, it was almost impossible *not* to get a loan. Home appraisals were adjusted to meet the amount needed to obtain a loan. All these new loans were then bundled and sold to banks, and pension funds all over the world that also shortcut their due-diligence process. Business and the economy were booming, and everyone was getting rich from this novel new way of financing home purchases. That is, until the people who were never underwritten, who should never have been given a loan to begin with, could not make their loan payments. Then the whole house of cards came crashing down.

The economic collapse has been well documented, but what is not well known is that Palmer & Cay, under the new management, was there first. We had a novel new way of producing business by shortcutting the traditional sales process of finding and attracting new clients. The plan was to let the other guys do all the hard work of building their business before we would swoop in and hire away the people, their accounts coming with them. In order to work our plan, we would overleverage the company betting on the come.

So you see, like the mortgage companies, we had a new way of doing business, and we sold our plan to the bank. And just like the housing crisis, we were overleveraged and could not make our payments. And like the housing crisis, many innocent people would have their lives disrupted because of all the "smart" people running the show.

Greed and debt in the stock market caused the Great Depression in the 1920s. Greed and debt caused the housing bubble to burst in the late 2000s. In between those two cataclysmic events, greed and debt sunk the Palmer Cay.

Epilogue

Palmer & Cay, founded in 1868, was 135 years old when the new people—board members and president—joined the company, and 137 years old when it went out of existence. From start to finish, it took the new management less than twenty-three months to destroy a company that had existed for over a century and a third. It would have been hard to have accomplished a quicker result if one was actually trying to reach the same outcome.

Unfortunately, the story of Palmer & Cay is more common in the business world than one would guess. It happens to companies of all sizes; just ask the people at Seagram's, or Kodak, or Enron, or any of the hundreds of .com companies that are no longer around. How does this happen? It is almost always human error, typically caused by people who, for lack of judgment, ethics, or ability, should never have been in charge. These people somehow work their way into positions of authority and, when left unchecked, cause extensive damage.

There was one last petty insult for the average shareholder of Palmer & Cay. When the funds were not distributed right away after the closing, I contacted Wachovia HR in Charlotte to see where the money was. I was told that the four big shareholders—John Cay, two board members, and Jim Meathe—had all received their money, but the rest would get theirs in around a week. Once again, no one was looking after the minority shareholders. It was every man for himself.

After the sale, Palmer & Cay was immediately folded into Wachovia Insurance Services, which was the insurance arm of Wachovia Bank out of Charlotte, North Carolina. As might be expected, Palmer & Cay people immediately began leaving. Some went to competitors while others searched around for smaller entrepreneurial firms where they could make a difference and have the freedom and income they deserved. Ironically, the few who stayed benefited from those who left. As people were leaving, any accounts they could not get to move with them were reassigned to those who stayed. Some people improved their income significantly without the hard work of finding new clients.

Atlanta Benefits Division

Shortly after the acquisition by Wachovia, I began getting feedback that the manager of the Atlanta Benefits Division—the one I was not allowed to compete with—was inexplicably not managing. He held some meetings, but there was no personal involvement with the troops on his part. At the time that seemed odd; however, two years later the answer came when he left the company, taking with him a group of employees and much of his business. He certainly proved to be smarter than I was, because he got paid twice for his business: once from Wachovia, and then an increase when First Union Bank bought Wachovia. He then left with much of his business to start his own company. When the bank went after him for violating his nonpiracy agreement, he settled with Wachovia for pennies on the dollar.

Wachovia Bank

Three years after acquiring Palmer & Cay, Wachovia Bank was in trouble as a result of the housing bubble. At the time, Wachovia was the sixth-largest US bank by assets, with a market value of around $21.6 billion. Only one minor problem: they had a $122 billion portfolio of option adjustable-rate mortgages that the CEO, Robert Steel, classified as "distressed." From what I had seen on the insurance side, I was not surprised that there were problems in mortgage banking. Needless to say, Wachovia was in trouble, resulting with Wells Fargo & Co., whose value at the time was $123.4 billion, stepping in and buying Wachovia. What remained of Palmer & Cay became part of Wells Fargo Insurance Services. To this day, there are a few holdovers from Palmer & Cay at Wells Fargo; however, maybe not enough to field a softball team.

John Cay

John stayed at Wachovia after the sale to try to pursue business with the same enthusiasm as before, hoping to have a major role in the insurance organization. Some people speculated that he just needed justification to write off the company jet that he purchased for $4 million as part of the sale of Palmer & Cay. It became evident fairly early on that Wachovia had no plan for him, and sometime thereafter it reduced his compensation dramatically. Could it be that Karen Lehman, as CFO of Wachovia Insurance Services, got her revenge when putting together the compensation plan for the budget? Just saying.

John married a woman in South Carolina and now lives in downtown Charleston. I'm not sure what John is doing these days; he could be helping his son Jack with the new Palmer & Cay.

Jack Cay

That's right, the new Palmer & Cay! Somewhere along the line, Jack left the bank and formed a new independent insurance-brokerage firm. The rumor I heard from a former Palmer & Cay manager is that when Jack asked his father to see about buying the name back from the bank, the answer was "No problem, you can have it for free. It's not worth anything." I never tried to verify that story because the magic is gone; there will never be another Palmer & Cay like the original.

Christopher Cay

Christopher moved back to Savannah, started a family, and started his own insurance agency, Cay Insurance Services, selling personal-lines insurance (homeowners and automobile) and small commercial accounts. From everything I hear, he is doing well, even expanding to other communities. He is definitely past the start-up phase, and I anticipate Christopher to be very successful.

Jim Meathe

Palmer & Cay was Jim's last job in the insurance business. Working with a partner, he is now building homes in the Atlanta area. I guess that's a fitting occupation for someone who owned three primary residences in Atlanta at the same time.

Gussenhoven and Platt

No one that I have been in contact with has heard of or seen either of the two board members. Now that I think about it, it was the same way when they were on the board of Palmer & Cay.

Mike Liss

Mike ended up moving his family back to Chicago shortly after everything settled down. He went to work for Willis, the company that basically saved Palmer & Cay from total destruction. I believe he is still there.

Bill Lenhart

Funny story about the twists life can take. Aon, the large insurance broker, tried to recruit Mike Liss as Palmer & Cay was going under. Mike talked to them and decided not to join. Back at the office, he mentioned the position to Bill Lenhart, who immediately called Aon to let them know he was interested. I guess he may have been in panic mode since his mentor, Jim Meathe, was out of the insurance business. Bill did get that job. In the time since those days, Bill has held at least four positions with at least three different companies, one of them twice. For those who are counting, that amounts to a different job every 2.75 years on average, which is just a little longer than his time with Palmer & Cay.

Joe Rogers

Probably the most interesting and outlandish of all the stories since the Palmer & Cay days, as corroborated by the *Atlanta Journal*, the *Atlanta Business Chronicle*, and all the major TV news outlets in Atlanta, is about this former Palmer & Cay board member and head of Waffle House Corporate. Joe divorced his longtime wife and sometime later married again. As a very wealthy person, Joe and his wife lived in Buckhead and had a personal assistant. I believe the assistant first worked for Joe's wife and then ultimately for Joe. Eventually, the relationship between the two became physical. The descriptions in the press were a lot more salacious than what I am writing here. Like affairs will do, things turned out bad, with the assistant having hard feelings. She went to a lawyer and they had her secretively film or record some of the relationship.

That is when the assistant and her lawyers should have called me for advice; however, they did not know to do that. What would I have told them? Having worked with Waffle House Corporate for fifteen years, I would have explained that Joe would not be threatened by legal action and would fight every case to a conclusion. That is exactly what happened, and to top things off,

Joe had his attorneys sue the assistant's attorneys and tried to have them disbarred for attempted blackmail.

Besides the entertainment value, what I found so interesting about this case—and why everyone in Atlanta followed it—was the persona of Joe Rogers. Joe was always known as a buttoned-up straight shooter. He was physically fit, worked hard, and was absolutely demanding of all those around him. This scandal was totally out of sync with his image. Maybe he had been distracted as Palmer & Cay was going down.

Don Chapman

The other board-member friend of John's has not been as easy to keep track of as Joe since the Palmer & Cay days. Once in a while his name or picture shows up in the press, usually in conjunction with a charity or his alma mater, Georgia Tech.

Tom Bennett

Tom is still with the firm he moved to after he left Palmer & Cay. They were acquired by the bank BB&T but, unfortunately, Tom missed that big bump because it happened before he joined. We have had the pleasure of working on a common client for many years and see each other several times a year. Although he has been successful at his current situation he, like me, wishes the Palmer & Cay we knew were still around.

Bill Stanton

Bill was a great professional and true gentleman who deserved more than what he got from Palmer & Cay. Unfortunately, shortly after retirement he became ill and passed away.

Ron Collins

My story is not so different from many you may have already heard. The year 2005 turned out to be especially difficult for our family. Of the five most stressful events a person can encounter, our family experienced at least four incidents. It started with my job change, then one of the children was diagnosed with a permanent health condition, then our beloved yellow Labrador retriever, Sophie, died, and finally Jeannie had a health scare that resulted in surgery. We were glad to put the year behind us.

After turning down overtures from Willis at the end of Palmer & Cay, I talked with several other companies, including an insurance company looking for a president of their Georgia corporation. I had given so much of myself in the sixteen years I was at Palmer & Cay that I just could not see myself back in a corporate executive role. However, there was a family-owned actuarial consulting firm that I almost joined before going to work at Palmer & Cay sixteen years earlier. I gave them a call and, after brief negotiations, they welcomed me into the firm. Unfortunately, the synergy between retirement planning and group insurance never developed as I had hoped, probably as much my fault as anything.

After almost two years, I partnered up with another Palmer & Cay refugee who was starting his own firm. His background was in commercial insurance, and the hope was that working together we could offer clients a complete package. After several years, what we discovered was that we each were only working on accounts we produced individually and there was no cross selling. Seeing no need to drive across town to work on my own accounts, we parted ways. Since then, I have been an independent insurance broker working out of an office in a high-rise building in Buckhead.

Cast of Characters

Frank Beard – Executive in charge of Commercial Insurance Division of Palmer & Cay; acting head of Atlanta office

Tom Bennett – Atlanta producer and only nonmanagement board member

Christopher Cay – Youngest son of John

Jack Cay – Oldest son of John and head of New York office; became last president of Palmer & Cay

John Cay – Chairman and primary owner of Palmer & Cay

John Carswell – Former owner of Carswell Company who joined Marsh

Don Chapman – Palmer & Cay board member; business owner; close friend of John Cay

Tom Coker – Administrative vice president of Atlanta Palmer & Cay office

Ron Collins – Author of this book; former senior vice president/managing partner in Atlanta office

Mike Crowley – Former president of Palmer & Cay who became vice chairman

Bill Danish – Atlanta benefits consultant; initial contact for merging KPMG offices in Atlanta, Washington, DC, and Baltimore

John Gussenhoven – New board member brought in by John Cay; formerly with Marsh

David Hofele – Chief legal counsel of Palmer & Cay

Don Holmes – Head of Denver office of Palmer & Cay

Doug Hutcherson – Atlanta producer who left leading thirteen others to join competitor Lockton Insurance

Karen Lehman – Former Palmer & Cay chief financial officer who became CFO of Wachovia Insurance Services

Bill Lenhart – National sales manager brought in by Jim Meathe

Mike Liss – Manager of Atlanta office who moved from Chicago

Phil Maddox – Atlanta producer; president of Piedmont Driving Club

Jim Meathe – President of Palmer & Cay; brought in after being fired from Marsh

Mel Mendenhall – Producer snatched away from Marsh at last minute

Fran Millar – Atlanta producer; Georgia politician, first in the State House of Representatives and then the State Senate

Dave Morgan – Benefits Division coleader of Palmer & Cay

Ron Norelli – Business consultant who Wachovia sent to analyze Palmer & Cay

Lew Oden – Retired executive vice president who helped build Palmer & Cay

Joe Platt – New board member brought in by John Cay; formerly with Marsh

Joe Rogers – Palmer & Cay board member; primary owner of Waffle House Corporate; close friend of John Cay

Fred Schrimp – Friend of Ron Collins who introduced Palmer & Cay to the CKE account, largest in Atlanta office
Ray Slabaugh – Benefits Division coleader of Palmer & Cay
Bill Stanton – Manager of Washington, DC, benefits practice
Will Underwood – Atlanta producer

Appendix

Lessons Learned

There are so many lessons to be learned from this calamity that it's hard to place them in order of importance. Thus, I will lay them out for you to triage.

Haste does make waste. As the old proverb suggests, when you try to speed things up by employing shortcuts, you often make a mess of things and in the long run come up short. When John Cay took over his father's insurance agency, the company had around $2 million in annual revenue. When Palmer & Cay bought the Carswell Company, the company was around $3.5 million and Carswell was larger at nearly $4.5 million, for a combined total of $8 million. In twenty years, the company went from approximately $8 million in annual revenue to nearly $150 million. Like the hedgehog theory in Jim Collins's book *Good to Great*, the growth was accelerating by doing what we were good at over and over again. We were good at two things: attracting and servicing clients, and buying and integrating other insurance firms.

We were already doing it the right way when John brought in the two outside board members, and then, together, they brought in the new president. They had convinced John that with their help, the company could quickly get to $300 million and soon thereafter $500 million. For that forecast, they were to get an ownership position in the company. If it failed, they would still each walk away with $5 million. There was no incentive *not* to be reckless. That deal alone should have sent up red flags. The only legitimate way we could have reached those goals in the time frame they were talking about was to get financial backing to make larger acquisitions. There never was a shortcut.

Ethics do matter. Unethical activity often produces short-term gains, only to have them come crashing down in the long run. At the time, it may seem unfair that people can get ahead by living on the edge, such as is often the case with politicians and athletes. However, there are many politicians in jail and many athletes who will not be enshrined into the Hall of Fame for their sport. So, was the new business plan ethical? You decide. It certainly was borderline at best. The whole approach adopted at Palmer & Cay for the last two years seemed wrong. What the new management was trying to do was take advantage of all the time, money, and energy expended by our competition to obtain clients. They wanted to walk in once the hard part was done and acquire the business by hiring away the people who had already been paid for producing that business.

To many of us, this plan did not feel right from the start. We would not like to lose business this way, and firms like Marsh or Aon could have crushed us using this method. So, why didn't they? Had the large firms violated the unwritten rule about wholesale raids on competitors, especially smaller ones, they would have faced antitrust regulations. Just because we were a small player did not excuse our behavior. Guess what? Clients get it. That's one reason the business never came over. That, and the fact that our management was hiring the wrong people. Most clients don't like to change advisers; doing so raises too many questions and has a certain amount of risk associated with it. The new, unproven concept was doomed from the start. We were not going from *Good to Great*, we were going in the other direction. It pains me to say we got what we deserved. Unfortunately, most of the many hardworking Palmer & Cay employees did not deserve to be caught up in the mess.

A number of us who had access to the information and were sophisticated enough to figure out what was going on could anticipate and, at least partially, prepare for the end results. There were many unaware people innocently going about their business who would be hurt both financially and career-wise as a result of the greed and stupidity at Palmer & Cay. There were a number of people, like Mike Liss, for example, who had rearranged their lives and moved families to new cities. They would be starting over a second time.

Did John Cay know what we were doing was wrong? You bet. Right before I cleaned out my desk at Palmer & Cay, the phone rang and Lew Oden was on the other end. I had not talked with Lew very often since he retired and was glad to hear from my old leader. He asked how I was doing, and we talked about different people we both knew in the industry. When the conversation got around to Palmer & Cay, Lew hit me with a stunner: "Ron, I had lunch with John in Savannah a while back, and he told me that he knew a month in that he had made a mistake. He did not think the difference in cultures would be as big of a deal as it turned out."

John always liked euphemisms, and "difference in cultures" was his way of saying right versus wrong. It was just not the business approach of these people. Many, if not most, of them spent their time thinking of ways for personal advancement rather than the job at hand of selling and servicing accounts. They would not let work get in the way of climbing the corporate ladder. These people were a product of their past environment. Their activities and approaches were part of what had driven many of us to leave the big, bureaucratic companies to begin with.

Several years later, in a discussion with the president of the second-largest independent insurance-brokerage firm in Georgia, I learned that he was introduced to Jim by John Cay at an industry meeting during the Meathe administration. At that introduction, John would not make eye contact, preferring to look down at his shoes before quickly walking away. Just another confirmation that John did know the truth and was having a hard time facing it. His Faustian bargain had been a terrible mistake.

A plan with poor execution is doomed. All plans, good or bad, must have the right execution in order to have a chance of success. The ill-conceived plan for dramatic growth at Palmer & Cay was dependent on stealing people from Marsh and Aon and, to a lesser degree, any other competitors in the insurance-brokerage business. So, who did the new management team go after? They recruited and hired anyone with "senior," "manager," or "VP" by their name. These were not necessarily the people with the strongest client contacts. Management loaded up the payroll with people who may or may not have been good insurance professionals. In any case, they were not the ones who could influence clients to change their loyalties. They added a great deal of expense with almost no additional revenue. Even if they had been able to lure the individuals with strong client relationships, I remain convinced that the process of bringing in enough new accounts would have outrun our money supply before we reached our goals. Changing third-party relationships is not a fast process, nor an easy one. Sometimes the client will only do it on renewal dates. Sometimes there are large ongoing claims that must be resolved before terminating agreements. Often the customer just won't move quickly. Many don't move at all.

A better plan would have been to take the $60 million that we borrowed from Wachovia and purchase a number of small agencies filling in the map in the Midwest. It would have taken a few more years to reach the $300 million threshold, but it would have been a heck of a lot safer for the company and the families of Palmer & Cay.

Be aware of empty suits. Actors often talk in a derogatory way about front-office suits, meaning the nonactor businessmen that run the studios. The same thing happens with athletes referring to management. An empty suit is a terrible thing that wastes time, money, and opportunity. The three men whom John brought in to take over the company, in my opinion as verified by the outcome, were not the right people to be effective in an entrepreneurial setting. They had been successful in advancing their careers in large, bureaucratic environments where the best way to get along is to go along. Over the years, much has been written about how individuals succeed in corporate America. A common theme is that the best way for an executive to advance is to not make enemies. The best way to not make enemies is to never take a strong stance. When management looks to promote, they tend to look for disqualifiers as a way to whittle down the field. That's why Marsh forced Jim Meathe out when he became so disruptive. His actions at Marsh made him expendable, no matter his business success.

John was many times better suited to lead than the men he brought into our environment. He was the visionary who led the company to its highest level. He was a tireless worker consumed by his goals. And, for the most part, he really was the level-five leader described in *Good to Great*, a concept that was poo-pooed by Jim Meathe. John was always generous in handing off business that he produced and always heaped praise on others. He knew what it took to be a successful executive. So, what happened?

John had one blind spot that is often found in leaders of all types. He tended to listen to outsiders more than the people in his own organization. And he did not have a "no" person in the firm except Lew Oden, who was long gone. Lew was the only one who really cracked the code on dealing with John. However, even Lew found it exhausting to keep fending off terrible ideas. Then, with Lew gone, those of us in management who tried to reign things in from time to time had limited success. Accordingly, when Gussenhoven made contact with John on another issue, he sensed a chance to become involved with Palmer & Cay. As I said before, he had nothing to lose, so why not roll the dice with someone else's money? I was told that during the transaction to sell the company to Wachovia, someone—I believe it was either Frank Beard or Mike Crowley before he left—proposed to Gussenhoven, Platt, and Meathe that maybe they should share some of their $5 million with the employees of the company since they were responsible for the downfall. Their response was a predictable rebuke: "That can come out of John's money." I was not surprised. I witnessed Jim Meathe blaming John for everything right up to the end. In my mind, the plan was not legitimate to begin with, and these men had no shame.

Business models are useful tools but not fixed formulas. They need to be observed, adjusted, and modified to address the changing shoals when navigating the business environment. It is a false assumption and lazy thinking to think the model is achieved by its description. Its description is not the achievement. The model is an aspiration, not a destination. When you describe the model as a destination, then you skip the need to do basic blocking and tackling. That is magical thinking. You think if you believe hard enough, then something will come into being without doing the spade work to prepare the garden. Of all his faults, Jim Meathe's worst and most galling was his magical thinking. Jim was living in an alternate universe that was not real and never would be.

Unfortunately, Jim was willing to take the company all the way and go down with The Ship, regardless of what that might mean for the careers of Palmer & Cay employees and their families.

Business is a competition, but it is not just a game. Competition in commerce makes for better products, services, and prices. Plus, the thrill of winning is a lot of fun. But business is not about just keeping score, whether that be in revenues, compensation, or titles. A company's lasting legacy is the products and services it provided and the purposeful meaning that activity gives to the lives of its owners and employees. The focus should always be on the meaning of what you are doing. In our business, that meant providing better coverage at lower costs for companies and their hardworking people. If you get that right, the rest will follow. When Palmer & Cay's new management lost sight of that meaning, it steered into a fog from which it never returned.

Don't bet the ranch after age forty-five. Ted Turner, the famous Georgia billionaire and founder of CNN, was known for betting the whole company on different ideas or business schemes. However, once he reached a certain age, he decided he would no longer take the long shots. He did not need to take the risks at an age when time would run out for a recovery. John Cay was around fifty-seven when he brought in the outsiders, and around fifty-nine when we sold the company. Had we gone totally bankrupt, he would not have had enough time to start all over. It would not have been the grand retirement he enjoys today with a private jet, home in downtown Charleston, and a plantation in South Carolina across the from the Savannah River. I had once encouraged John to terminate the three amigos and not honor their contracts. Contract or not, a good lawyer could figure out how to stop the madness. Maybe we could have hired a sports attorney; they seem to know how to break contracts. The recklessness demonstrated by these men, especially Jim Meathe's disregard for contracts, may have been enough to win over a court. I think John's pride kept him from taking action. It is hard for someone so public to let the world know in court how wrong he was, how he got taken by these outsiders, or how he let greed and ego blind him. Pride can be expensive.

What was the final cost? In the end, after paying off debt, I believe we may have received somewhere under $200 million for a company with $140 million of revenue. Although we all suffered the same low share price, the sheer volume held by John was a fortune. John's total after the sale may have been as much as $90 million. He could withstand the disaster and move on comfortably while the rest of us lost valuable ground, some of us at an age when we should have been planning for retirement. Had we sold two years earlier before changing our business model, we probably would have sold for between $280 million and $420 million. That was an expensive twenty-four months.

In the process, John lost something very important to him: his reputation as a business leader. John had seen himself as a mover and shaker. He belonged to all the right clubs, social groups, and industry organizations. People were always trying to get in to see him for his input or to pitch an idea. Now, the magic was gone; those days were over. I remember how uneasy I felt when I heard a remark from a partner in an equity firm we had worked with for years. When told that Wachovia was buying Palmer & Cay, he said, "Yeah, I heard John finally found someone to take the company off his hands." That lack of respect bothered me.

At one time, we really did have "the magic." To this day, years later, two or more former Palmer & Cay people cannot get together without the conversation turning to how good things were back in the day. What we had will not be replaced. Many of our former associates have moved on with their lives, a number becoming very successful. However, there is no way to put lightning back in the Palmer & Cay bottle.

There was no integration plan. Once the bank got ahold of us, there never was a plan other than the personnel guidelines provided by the bank. Those guidelines were appropriate for managing thousands of bank tellers and behind-the-scenes employees; however, they were totally lacking for highly educated and trained insurance professionals, especially those working directly with clients. It was like asking Ferrari mechanics to do maintenance on school buses. On top of the stifling bank regulations, it was obvious that the executives in charge of the insurance division did not have the background or experience for merging financial-service organizations. And by all appearances, they didn't much care.

So, what are the consequences of a poorly managed acquisition? The answer can be found in a statement from my first boss in the insurance-brokerage business: "In financial services, a good acquisition is when you can retain at least fifty percent of the employees and fifty percent of the accounts." I am not sure how much of Palmer & Cay was retained by Wachovia, but I would be very surprised if it was that high. Essentially, all the good will that Wachovia paid for went right down the drain. No one seemed to care. In a conversation with an in-house bank attorney, I learned that when people left Wachovia and violated their nonpiracy agreements, the bank would sue or threaten to sue before settling for twenty-five cents on the dollar. You would think there would have been a cohesive plan to retain as many people and accounts as possible, yet there seemed to be a ho-hum attitude as if they were buying a manufacturing plant instead of a sophisticated financial-services firm. The merger was somehow "just going to happen." Oh, they held meetings, but those were mostly to tell you what you couldn't do when working for a bank. As expected, over the next few years people rushed for the exits.

There was an interesting casualty of the rules and regulations. A group of minority employees asked to meet with the new head of the Atlanta region. I guess they figured that since he was a minority, they would be in a good position. A lunch was arranged for a group of around twelve people led by a longtime female Palmer & Cay employee. While the group was munching on salads, the bank was running background checks on all employees. A few weeks later, the meeting organizer was called into HR and fired. Evidently, there was something in her past from many years before that did not pass muster with the bank. She had been a Palmer & Cay employee for over a decade; however, as they say at the bank, "Rules are rules."

About the Author

Ron Collins, CLU, FLMI, is a thirty-year-plus veteran of the insurance industry with twenty-five years of management experience. The majority of his career has been in the stewardship of employee-benefits plans for clients throughout the United States. During his career, he has been the recipient of numerous sales and management awards.